Judicial Corporal Punishment as an Alternative to Incarceration in the United States

Judicial Corporal Punishment as an Alternative to Incarceration in the United States

Lessons Learned from Islamic Criminal Justice Systems

Sanaz Alasti

Foreword by
Mitchel P. Roth

LEXINGTON BOOKS
Lanham • Boulder • New York • London

Published by Lexington Books
An imprint of The Rowman & Littlefield Publishing Group, Inc.
4501 Forbes Boulevard, Suite 200, Lanham, Maryland 20706
www.rowman.com

86-90 Paul Street, London EC2A 4NE

British Library Cataloguing in Publication Information Available

Library of Congress Cataloging-in-Publication Data Available

ISBN 978-1-66693-029-0 (cloth)
ISBN 978-1-66693-030-6 (ebook)

This book is dedicated to my father, Hossein Alasti,
mentor of a lifetime and a friend, and to my mother,
Maliheh Bahramizadeh for her support and love.
Without their support,
none of my advanced legal studies and my academic
accomplishments would have been possible!

Contents

List of Figures and Tables

FIGURES

TABLES

Foreword

By Mitchel P. Roth

In 1994, the caning of an eighteen-year-old expatriate named Michal Fay in Singapore aroused international censure, mostly from Western countries. Fay had been charged with fifty-three counts of vandalism, two of mischief and one charge of possessing stolen property. What outraged human rights activists most was his sentence of four months in jail, a USD 2,500 fine, and six strokes of cane (reduced to four under appeal). While Singapore was roundly excoriated by human rights groups in the Western world, the country did not back down, and Fay was caned along with nine other prisoners. The prisoners were stripped naked by prison authorities, bent over with their arms and legs fastened to an H-shaped framework with straps, and their kidneys were shielded for protection. Fay and the others, after shaking hands with the caner, were able to return to their cells without aid. Although Islamic justice came under fire for this punishment, what was mostly lost on observers was the fact that Singapore's legal system is rooted in English common law (like the United States). British imperialists introduced caning in the 1820s, and after its independence in 1965 Singapore retained corporal punishment in its legal code. Indeed, whipping with a birch had been a feature of British colonial judicial systems for almost two hundred years. This form of corporal punishment became so identified with the British that the French dubbed it "The English Vice." It was not until 1998 that British MPs voted to abolish the punishment.

Islamic criminal justice systems have been the object of increasing research in recent years, particularly from a comparative historical perspective. This is especially true when it comes to comparisons with Western criminal justice practices. The legal scholar Sanaz Alasti in her new book *Judicial Corporal Punishment as an Alternative to Incarceration in the United States: Lessons Learned from Islamic Criminal Justice Systems* takes a novel and thought-provoking approach to examining corporal punishment as an alternative to imprisonment in various historical contexts. This tome is the product of more than a decade of research on corporal and capital punishment. This author is ideally placed to undertake this research project, having made the transition from being a legal scholar and lawyer in Iran to her current role as a criminal justice professor and director of the Center for Death Penalty Studies at Lamar University in Beaumont, Texas. Her familiarity with both Islamic and Western criminal justice systems inspired her to make this comparative study. She utilized the United States as a prism for examining Western criminal justice practices, and likewise, uses Iran as her template for looking at Islamic criminal justice.

This book examines the implementation of corporal punishment as a potential alternative to imprisonment. It is unique for suggesting that corporal punishment can be viewed as an alternative to prison alongside such more modern alternatives as restorative justice and reintegrative and community practices. Moreover, Alasti suggests that considering penological practices in some parts of the world, corporal punishment might be a less cruel alternative to spending years behind bars in primitive and punitive jails and prisons. While she does not suggest this should be the norm, the author does present an intriguing question—"which is more barbaric?"

The author begins the book by chronicling the histories of corporal punishment in America and Iran, from their earliest eras to the present. Focus is given to the contemporary usage of corporal punishment and examines the wide variety of corporal punishment measures. This book dispels the notion that one criminal justice system is better than another and suggests that good practices can be found in Islamic and Western systems. While Islamic punishments have historically been portrayed as cruel and unusual by Western observers, the same holds true for Islamic observers of American criminal justice practices, which includes locking up a larger percentage of the population than most other countries in the world, Iran included.

As far back as the Ottoman Empire (1453–1922), an Islamic multinational state rarely matched in history, European travelers reported a legal system that demanded swift justice that compared favorably with European legal practices, which by contrast were often long-drawn-out affairs. Still other travelers brought back tales of hasty executions and cruel punishments. Although corporal punishment has its supporters in some Western countries, human rights supporters and activists have made sure that corporal punishments can only be regarded in the pejorative sense. The United States is still coming to terms with alternatives to imprisonment, and there is little support for reverting back to colonial practices reflecting common law. However, in 1979 Iran conversely reverted back to *Sharia* law, which ratcheted up its penal sanctions. Legal systems are constantly changing, influenced by other justice systems, geopolitics, and current history. Alasti makes a number of provocative observations and through her adoption of comparative historical research methodologies casts new light on the potential uses and abuses of corporal punishments.

Mitchel, P. Roth, PhD
Professor of Criminal Justice and Criminology
Sam Houston State University

Introduction

During my experience as a professor of criminal justice, after more than a decade of conducting research on harsh punishments in the secular and religious criminal justice systems, I developed my research on the issues related to the effectiveness of shock punishments. The research helped me to understand many views that non-scholars do not have. I conducted research about the cruelty of capital punishment. Later, I developed my research on the origin of judicial corporal punishments.

In this book, I ask if judicial corporal punishment might be a justifiable form of punishment. I shall argue that incarceration is a justifiable method of punishment, but the prison system is both expensive and lacking efficacy. A number of academics in the Western world defend certain forms of corporal punishment, but the review of the contemporary experience of Islamic criminal justice systems proves if it is a deterrent or not. Also, since certain types of corporal punishment cannot be administered without humiliating the offender, this book explains if it is in violation of human rights, and it should be abolished.

We are in a time when the US history of incarceration is being questioned, and alternatives are being considered. So, in a way, this book is timely. Typically, alternatives being considered are on the side of community/reintegrative/restorative processes. This book takes a different approach and examines the alternative of a seemingly archaic, physical (but non-carceral) punishment—corporal punishment. Although much has been written regarding corporal punishment in schools, this book is unique in examining corporal punishment as a form of punishment in contemporary criminal justice systems. The thesis this book explores is this: retaining judicial corporal punishment is a good solution for contemporary criminal justice systems, and it is more effective compared to incarceration. The purpose of this book, therefore, is to analyze this claim that judicial corporal punishment represents a more deterrent, less costly, and more humane alternative to incarceration. In evaluating this assertion, the book focuses on the example of judicial corporal punishment as implemented in Islamic criminal justice systems. This book compares corporal punishment as a form of cruel and unusual punishment in Western societies (represented by the United States) and Islamic societies (represented by Iran). This study seeks to provide taxpayers and policymakers with information about the policy behind judicial corporal punishment and if it could help significantly reduce the financial costs of imprisonment.

Surprisingly, little research has been done focusing on this issue, or they are far from comprehensive. Therefore, I have undertaken to correct this problem. Most of the books already published in this area deal primarily with the history of judicial corporal punishment or have been published by Western pro-corporal punishment scholars. In this book, I have closely and critically analyzed this topic using a comparative historical approach, which distinguishes this book from other published works. This book compares corporal punishment as a form of cruel and unusual punishment in Western societies (represented by the United States) and Islamic societies (represented by Iran). This enabled me to produce a very comprehensive work.

Although judicial corporal punishment has not been carried out in the United States in seventy years and has not been seriously discussed by any state legislature for nearly thirty years, by considering the strong support for judicial corporal punishment from a vocal minority of American scholars, it is my opinion that writing a book and making the case against the return of corporal punishment in the United States has become necessary. The book is both lively and thought-provoking for the practitioners and represents a useful contribution to the literature on the subject.

In writing this book, I have many readers in mind including the general public, students of law, criminal justice, criminology and sociology, as well as policy makers. The issue of finding an alternative to incarceration is one that always catches the attention of the general public and, of course, the media. Anytime that somebody is sentenced to corporal punishments such as flogging or amputation of hand in Islamic criminal justice systems, public reaction is enormous and triggers serious debates on these issues. In light of this, I have written this highly authoritative and comprehensive book for this wide range of readers.

All literature regarding judicial corporal punishments in the United States and Islamic law has been reviewed before completing this book. This book will be an excellent sourcebook for both undergraduate and graduate students in the field of law, criminal justice, criminology, and sociology. This book provides an up-to-date, comprehensive, and comparative examination of the concept of cruel and unusual punishment in both Western and Islamic societies.

Another issue is the following: does corporal punishment constitute a form of cruel and unusual punishment? The condemnation of cruel and unusual punishment is universal, but what exactly constitutes cruel and unusual punishment is highly subjective in both national and international law. The American concept of cruel and unusual punishment is traceable to early English history (English Bill of Rights). The prohibition against cruel and unusual punishment in the English Bill of Rights restricted the imposition of an excessive degree of punishment. Upon introduction to North America, the concept took an expanded meaning, and emphasis was placed on restricting the kind of punishment that might be imposed. The Eighth Amendment to the US Constitution provides that "cruel and unusual punishments" shall not be inflicted.

This provision is applicable to the states through the Due Process Clause of the Fourteenth Amendment, and similar provisions exist in some state constitutions. While some state constitutional provisions are held to be of identical scope to that of the Eighth Amendment, other provisions are deemed to afford greater protection than their federal counterpart.

When discussing punishment in Islamic criminal justice systems, one must keep in mind that the relationship between the state and the concept of justice is derived from the religious principle of Islam. The sharia, general and particular rules of Islamic corpus juris, is not merely a code of law but a code of conduct of behavior and ethics, a combination of law and morality, one and inseparable. Evidence of this relationship can be seen in the Penal Code of Iran which imposes the death penalty and corporal punishments on a variety of crimes.

Throughout history, varying punishments were deemed cruel and unusual, including surgical castration, vasectomies, and certain forms of the death penalty. The exact meaning of the concept has vacillated from decade to decade, court to court, and place to place. The meaning of "cruel and unusual" must draw from the evolving standards of decency that mark the progress of a maturing society. The test, then, will ordinarily be a cumulative one: If a punishment is unusually severe, if there is a strong probability that it is inflicted arbitrarily, if it is substantially rejected by contemporary society, and if there is no reason to believe that it serves any penal purpose more effectively than some less severe punishment, then the continued infliction of that punishment violates the idea that the state may not inflict inhuman and uncivilized punishments upon those convicted of crimes.

The primary aim of this book is to demonstrate that harshness in the law of punishment such as corporal punishment, long sentences of imprisonment, and harshness in the inflexibility of punishment (applying unvarying punishments regardless of any sense of the individual deserts of offenders) contradicts with the Universal Declaration of Human Rights and every other law concerning this matter.

Another aim of this book is to use a comparative historical approach in illustrating the similarities and differences in cruel and unusual punishments over time and place. In order to achieve this aim, the history of judicial corporal punishment, an analysis of judicial corporal punishment across the world and whether it has spread in popularity or has slowly declined, and finally the current practices of corporal punishments in both Iran and United States have been critically reviewed. Through this comparative historical perspective, the reader can gain appreciation of the Western and Islamic nature of these punishment practices.

This book is organized in six chapters. Chapter 1 focuses on the history of corporal punishment and the definition of what constitutes a judicial corporal punishment. Chapter 1 has three sections: defining judicial corporal punishment, history of corporal punishment at the national level using the United States and Iran as examples.

Chapter 2 focuses on the universal purposes of punishment and follows with a comparative analysis of judicial corporal punishments as an alternative to incarceration under the United States and Islamic criminal justice systems. It examines different scholarly debates regarding this issue.

Chapter 3 claims whipping could potentially serve retribution, rehabilitation, and deterrence objectives. However, the evidence concerning whether whipping is an effective form of specific deterrence is inconclusive. Considering many factors, I explain if judicial corporal punishment can meet with the penological and philosophical challenge of just punishment and can also go much of the way to solving the fiscal problem of criminal punishment or merely represents the "essence of barbarism."

Chapter 4 explains different methods of corporal punishment in the United States and Islamic criminal justice systems such as whipping, branding, mutilation, docking stool and stocks, and pillory. Also, it discusses how international treaties and applying international law norms in domestic courts can limit the use of corporal punishments. It outlines the background of prohibition of cruel and unusual punishment under International Conventions from the Convention Against Torture and Other Cruel, Inhuman, or Degrading Treatment or Punishment, the Universal Declaration of Human Rights, the International Covenant on Civil and Political Rights, the African Charter, and the American Convention of Human Rights.

At the beginning of the twenty-first century, corporal punishment is no longer a legal sanction in most countries around the world. At the same time, in some countries, corporal punishment has been reinstated and even extended. Chapter 5 is about abolitionist v. retentionist nations. This chapter examines the use of judicial corporal punishment as implemented under Islamic criminal justice systems.

Finally, the last chapter 6 explores whether corporal punishment violates human rights, and if it is a form of cruel and inhuman punishment based on numerous international human rights documents and cases.

Chapter 1

Definition and History of Corporal Punishment

> Corporal punishment is "A practice than which nothing tends more to harden and degrade"[1] vs. Corporal punishment may be reactionary, but it is better than nothing.[2]

WHAT IS JUDICIAL CORPORAL PUNISHMENT?

Corporal punishment was mild in comparison to other punishments of the era. The use of physical punishments has a history in nearly all cultures. Europeans used several forms of punishment intended either to inflict pain, to publicly humiliate offenders, or both. Branding, mutilation, the stock and pillory, the bilbo, the ducking stool, hard labor, and flogging were all used by the British government to punish criminals.

Judicial corporal punishment is almost nonexistent today in industrialized democratic countries, except for disciplining children in families and schools. Corporal punishment is the punishment of body. It is defined as "physical punishment as distinguished from pecuniary punishment or a fine; any kind of punishment of or inflicted on the body."[3]

The term corporal punishment is subject to different definitions. *Black's Law Dictionary* defines corporal punishment as "physical punishment, punishment that is inflicted upon the body."[4] Professor Geoffrey Scarre defines corporal punishments: "In the broad sense, any punishment inflicted on the body meant to cause physical pain, discomfort or injury counts as corporal."[5] Although this definition is broad, Scarre says "For the term corporal punishment to apply in the narrow sense, the pain or harm must be intentionally produced by an act of battery or assault."[6]

Corporal punishments are the most obvious acute punishments, but there are many kinds of corporal punishment, and not all have the same physical and mental effects. Most corporal punishments are discrete acts that visibly harm the offender's body. Their consequences are ordinarily foreseeable and clearly intended. Hence, the state's culpability is not in question.

Corporal punishments typically inflict readily apparent physical injuries, such as the lacerations caused by whippings. There are five degrees of corporal punishment: whipping—first degree; burning skin—second degree; mutilation—third degree; merciful death—fourth degree; and prolonged death—fifth degree.[7] The drafters of the Eighth Amendment intended to prohibit all but the first and fourth degrees.

Although in some definitions the death penalty is a form of corporal punishment, this book has adopted a narrow definition, and corporal punishment refers to physical harm to the body with or without serious risk of death. Thus, the death penalty is not included.

Also, nonjudicial corporal punishments for children or tribal corporal punishments are not included in this book. The term judicial qualifies the act of punishment as one duly sentenced by a court after a trial and guilt. As a judicial act, the presumption here is that corporal punishment complies with all constitutional provisions and the criminal justice system of a nation that prescribes the corporal punishment.

HISTORY OF CORPORAL PUNISHMENT IN THE UNITED STATES FROM COLONIAL TIMES TO TWENTIETH CENTURY

In colonial America, another category of punishments was bodily punishment. These punishments, which would later become known as corporal punishments, were directed at the body of the offender and intended to cause pain. Aware of the shocking apparatus of death and torment employed throughout the world at the time, colonial legislatures were concerned with establishing limits on the severity of these types of punishments. The Massachusetts Body of Liberties, which established the original capital laws of the colony, placed a restriction on bodily punishments by stating, "We allow amongst us none that are inhumane, barbarous, or cruel." A review of the bodily punishments commonly used in seventeenth-century America reflects the ideas of the day as to what was or was not barbarous, inhumane, and cruel.[8]

Corporal punishment was the most common form of punishment for no capital offenses in colonial America. Devices used for corporal punishment included the pillory, the whipping post, and the ducking stool. The corporal punishments inflicted upon offenders were public and highly ceremonial.

Colonists used public beatings to prevent recurrences of illegal or sinful conduct and to deter potential offenders from committing such crimes themselves. While the physical abuse was severe, the accompanying shame was often the most painful ingredient of the punishment.

> The sting of the lash and the contortions of the stocks were surely no balm, but even worse for community members were the piercing stares of neighbors who witnessed their disgrace and with whom they would continue to live and work.[9]

When corporal punishments dominated penal policy in the American colonies, sanctioning authorities often administered them for public viewing. Onlookers saw the body visibly marked and displayed. Punishment had become theater and education: "The large whipping-post painted red stood conspicuously and prominently on the most public street in Boston. It was placed in State Street directly under the windows of a great writing school which I frequented, and from there the scholars were indulged in the spectacle of all kinds of punishment suited to harden their hearts and brutalize their feelings. Here women were tied to the post with bare backs on which thirty or forty lashes were bestowed among the screams of the culprit and the uproar of the mob."[10]

Corporal Punishment in Early America (1597–1740)

In Virginia and Southern colonies, from its earliest days colonial authorities relied on brutal corporal punishments. For instance, a Virginian colonist was severely punished for making false charges against another colonist. As punishment, the offender was sentenced to be disarmed and have his arm broken and his tongue bored through with an awl and was then forced to walk through a gauntlet of forty men and battered by each one. In 1618, a more moderate law code was introduced, but there were few alternatives to the tradition of harsh corporal punishment. Public shaming or exhibitory punishments were often effective in curbing petty crime. Malefactors were forced to sit in the stocks or stand in the pillories or offer public penance in church for violating conventional moral standards. The ducking stool astride a prominent riverbank saw frequent use when women acted outside their traditional gender rules. Women who committed bastardy, or childbirth outside marriage and could not afford to pay a fine, were liable to be publicly whipped while naked to the waist. Since slaves were always a valuable commodity, mutilation, whipping, and other corporal punishment were administered quickly and visibly to set an example and not interfere with agricultural work.[11]

In Massachusetts and the New England colonies in lieu of the death penalty, several examples suggest that fines and whipping were the normal modes of punishment. Other public sanctions exposed offenders to an array of corporal punishments, including whipping, the stocks, and pillories. Whipping was administered for fornication. These punishments were administrated publicly before the assembled community, usually on the market, lecture, or military training day. Habitual drunkards wore the shame letter D, for drunkard, for an entire year. An unscrupulous baker sometimes stood in the stocks supporting a lump of dough on his head. Chronic property offenders were branded on the cheek or forehead or mutilated, living the mark of infamy to warn the community of their criminal disposition. Like the wearing of shame letters, which sent a message to the community, a specific form of maiming also sent a warning to potential miscreants. Among the more grotesque punishment administrated by Puritans were the amputation of ears, slitting of nostrils, and branding of faces and hands.[12]

In Pennsylvania and the Mid-Atlantic colonies, individuals arrested for civic disorder or physical violence were punished severely, particularly in rape cases. One individual facing the shame and the pain of a public whipping for rape slit his own throat before the sentence could be carried out. Whipping remained in fashion in Pennsylvania throughout the eighteenth century. Neighboring Delaware, heavily influenced by the early Quaker Code, even had a name for its permutation of this device known as "Red Hannah." Anachronistic Delaware authorities continued to whip prisoners into the 1940s.[13]

Corporal Punishment in Revolutionary Times (1718–1797)

The eighteenth century is often referred to as the Age of Reason, or the Enlightenment. During this era, great thinkers such as Beccaria, Bentham, Howard, and Penn had a great impact on the treatment of criminals. Their efforts resulted in the transition from corporal punishment to correction and laid the groundwork for the modern penitentiary. Beccaria harshly condemned the use of torture in punishment, the corruption of state officials, and disproportionality severe penalties for minor offenses.[14]

Corporal Punishment in the New Nation (1777–1857)

With population growth, increasing mobility, and migration, the emergence of a distinct poor population made sanctions such as fines, whipping, and the pillory less effective than in the past. While the use of capital punishment had diminished, corporal punishment was another matter, with many criminal offenses still being punished with the public infliction of pain and suffering. Most towns in New England boasted whipping posts and stocks near the commons or meetinghouse. As late as 1805, the penalty in Massachusetts for counterfeiting was the amputation of an ear after sitting in a pillory for an hour. "The penalty for manslaughter consisted of having one's forehead branded in public, and many communities flogged perpetrators of petty theft.[15] But by the 1830s, public corporal punishment began to disappear from statute books as prison became a more accepted sanction for most crimes. In 1790, Pennsylvania began the movement to prohibit flogging, and in 1805, Massachusetts followed suit. The movement to abolish corporal punishment was haphazard at best, with Connecticut constables continuing to whip petty criminals until 1828 and Delaware officials flogging black and white prisoners well into the twentieth century.[16]

Corporal Punishment in the Civil War Era (1856–1876)

Corporal punishment, with few exceptions, had all but disappeared by the Civil War.[17] Penal historians have attributed the near extinction of corporal punishment to three factors: (1) the new republic's eagerness to abandon old world criminal sanctions, one being corporal punishment; (2) "riotous disorder" in the nation's rapidly growing cities, resulting in a loss of confidence in the traditional mechanisms of social control; and (3) a new perspective on deviance that attributed criminality to a familial defect, a failure of upbringing.[18]

Corporal Punishment in the Young Nation

Gradually, criminal punishment in America evolved away from its emphasis on corporal and humiliating punishments until by the end of the first half of the nineteenth century, imprisonment was virtually the only method of criminal punishment used by most states besides capital punishment and monetary fine. This evolution can be attributed in large part to the birth of the modern science of penology.[19]

In the early days of post-colonies America, attempts to reform the severe Penal Code of England took place, and calls for further reform met eager ears. In 1793, in a pamphlet entitled "*An Enquiry How Far the Punishment of Death is Necessary in Pennsylvania*," William Bradford advanced the ideas of Beccaria and Montesquieu. In his introduction, Bradford cites these philosophers as the basis for three important propositions: the prevention of crimes is the sole end of punishment, every punishment which is not necessary for that purpose is a cruel and tyrannical act, and every penalty should be proportioned to the offense.[20]

Bradford argued that milder forms of punishment were as effective at curbing offenses as the most severe. He pointed to the lenient departure from the English penal system that William Penn orchestrated in the colony of

Pennsylvania between the years 1683 and 1718, when corporal punishment was replaced with prison. Bradford argued, "During this long space of thirty-five years, it does not appear that the mildness of the laws invited offenses, or that Pennsylvania was the theatre of more atrocious crimes than the other Colonies."[21]

Bradford also pointed to one of the major problems with a severe penal code, jury nullification, and related it to the writings of Montesquieu. Faced with the awesome responsibility of sending an individual to the gallows or some other heinous punishment, juries would often acquit if they felt sympathy for the prisoner. According to Bradford, "the unwillingness of witnesses to prosecute, the facility with which juries acquitted, and the prospects of pardon, created hopes of impunity which invited and multiplied the offense."[22]

HISTORY OF CORPORAL PUNISHMENT IN IRAN FROM THE ANCIENT TIMES TO THE REVOLUTIONARY RESTATEMENT OF CORPORAL PUNISHMENT

Corporal Punishment in the Ancient Era

In ancient Persia, punishments were harsh and in the majority of cases the death penalty was applied. Whipping under the Achaemenian[23] and Sassanian[24] dynasties was widely practiced. Punishment for poisoning shepherd dogs was two hundred lashes. In this era, whipping was a religious concept based on Zoroastrian[25] religion. When humans commit a crime, the devil exerts influence. Because the death penalty and imprisonment do not have any effect on the devil, the punishment is whipping. For this reason, whipping was an important punishment in Zoroastrian laws.[26]

In addition to whipping, mutilation, taking off the skin, scalding, branding, and shame punishments such as shaving the head, beard, and wearing wooden signs in public for months for petty crimes were practiced.[27]

Corporal Punishment in the Islamic Era

After the Islamic era, the criminal justice system of ancient Iran was replaced by Islamic laws. Muslims enforced Islamic criminal rules to establish order, security, and the promotion of Islam. After the invasion by the Arabs, corporal punishment was based on Islamic rules.[28] Islamic punishments were administrated up to the ratification of Penal Code in Iran, when the Pahlavi Dynasty replaced the Qajar Dynasty (1779–1925).

Corporal Punishment under the Pahlavi Monarchy (1925–1979)

Iran's secular criminal justice system was formed under the Pahlavi Dynasty and its two monarchs, Reza Shah (1925–1941) and Mohammad Reza Shah (1941–1979). Modern criminal law in Iran was based on modern capitalist notions of crime and punishment. The first Penal Code of Iran was ratified in 1926. Based on Iran's Penal Code, the only applicable corporal punishment was flogging for knife-stabbing,[29] vagrancy,[30] and gaining ownership of another person's property.[31] In 1966, Iran's parliament ratified the "Abolition of Flogging Statute," and after that time we have not observed any kind of corporal punishment in Pahlavi era.[32]

Corporal Punishment after the Islamic Revolution (1979)

The present criminal justice system in Iran regarding some punishments is based on the Twelve Imami Shii version of the *Sharia* law. This system formed in the early 1980s during the tenure of the Ayatollah Ruhullah Mosavi Khomeini. In 1983, the first specific Islamic Penal Statute was ratified. The Statute of Retaliation prescribed punishments such as flogging, mutilation, and shame for those crimes with fixed punishment in the Holy Quran and tradition. Therefore, for other crimes jurists refer to the modern Penal Code of Iran. In 1984, the discretionary punishment statute was ratified in Iran. Under this statute, flogging was considered as a punishment for sixty-four different crimes. Chapters two and three of the Islamic Penal Code outline retaliation and prescribed punishments ratified in 1992. Immediately after, chapter five of the Islamic Penal Code was ratified in 1997 (discretionary and preventive punishments). This statute also includes flogging for different crimes but the incidence of flogging decreased when compared to the 1984 statute.[33] (For more information please refer to chart 4.1 in chapter 4 and figure 3.1 in chapter 3.) Furthermore, Article 729 of this statute abolished all contrary statutes including the modern Penal Code of Iran.[34]

NOTES

1. Edmund Burke, The Annual Register, *Or A View of the History, Politics, and Literature for the Year 1817*, 566 (London: Baldwin Cradoack and Joy, 1818).
2. Fyodor Dostoyevsky, *Notes from Underground*. Dover Thrift Editions (Mineola, NY: Dover Publications, 1992).
3. Steven A. Hatfield, *Criminal Punishment in America: From the Colonial to the Modern Era, 1* USAFA J. Leg. Stud. 180 (1990).
4. *Black's Law dictionary,* 1353 (10th ed. 2014).

5. Geoffrey Scarre, *Corporal Punishment*, 6 Ethical Theory & Moral Prac. 296, 297, n.3 (2003).

6. *Id.*

7. Pieter Spierenburg, *The Body and the State, in The Oxford History of the Prison,* 49–53, Norval Morris & David J. Rothman eds. (1995).

8. Steven Hatfield, *supra* note 3, at 181.

9. Scott Sanders, *Scarlet Letters, Bilbo's and Cable TV: Are Shame Punishments Cruel and Unusual or are they Viable Option for American Jurisprudence?* 37 Washburn L.J. 359 (1998).

10. Anna Green Winslow, *Diary of Anna Green Winslow: A Boston School Girl of 1771* (Houghton Mifflin, 1895)

11. Mitchel P. Roth, *Crime and Punishment: A History of the Criminal Justice System*, 54–55 (Thomson Wadsworth, CA, 2005).

12. *Id*, at 55–56.

13. Robert Graham Caldwell, *Red Hannah, Delaware Whipping Post*, 69–82 (University of Philadelphia Press, 1947).

14. Mitchell Roth, *supra* note 11, at 89–90.

15. Id.

16. *Id*, at 110.

17. State and federal authorities, however, continued to inflict capital punishment. States conducted fifty-seven reported executions from 1864 to 1890. See Margaret Werner Cahalan, U.S. Department of Justice, Historical Corrections Statistics in the United States, 1850–1984, at 10 tbl.2-1 note a (1986). They carried out 155 reported executions in the 1890s. Whippings continued well into the twentieth century. See generally Robert Caldwell, Red Hannah: Delaware's Whipping Post (1947) (documented nearly three hundred years of whippings in Delaware). In some state prisons, whipping as a disciplinary sanction was practiced as late as the 1960s. Discussing changing judicial attitudes toward the whipping of inmates. See generally Graeme Newman, Just and Painful 7-8 (2d ed. 1995) (calling for a return to human corporal punishments for the majority of offenders who do not need to be locked away).

18. James Robertson, *Houses of the Dead: Warehouse Prisons, Paradigm Change, and the Supreme Court*, 34 Hous. L. Rev. 1003 (1997).

19. *Id.*

20. William Bradford, *An Enquiry How Far the Punishment of Death is Necessary in Pennsylvania*, 12 American Journal of Legal History 158. 18 U.S.C. 3567 (1968).

21. *Id.*

22. *Id.*

23. Achaemenian dynasty (559–330 BCE) was ancient Iranian dynasty whose kings founded and ruled the Achaemenian Empire. Probably the greatest of the Achaemenian rulers were Cyrus II (reigned 559–c.529 BCE), who actually established the empire and from whose reign it is dated; Darius I (522–486), who excelled as an administrator and secured the borders from external threats; and Xerxes I (486–465), who completed many of the buildings begun by Darius. During the time of Darius I and Xerxes I, the empire extended as far west as Macedonia and Libya and as far east

as the Hyphasis (Beās) River; it stretched to the Caucasus Mountains and the Aral Sea in the north and to the Persian Gulf and the Arabian Desert in the south.

24. Sassanian dynasty was ancient Iranian dynasty that ruled an empire (224–651 CE), rising through Ardashir I's conquests in 208–224 CE and destroyed by the Arabs during the years 637–651. Under the leadership of Ardashīr (reigned as "king of kings" 224–241), the Sasanians overthrew the Parthians and created an empire that was constantly changing in size as it reacted to Rome and Byzantium the west and to the Kushans and Hephthalites to the east. At the time of Shapur I (reigned 241–272), the empire stretched from Sogdiana and Iberia (Georgia) in the north to the Mazun region of Arabia in the south and extended to the Indus River in the east and to the upper Tigris and Euphrates river valleys in the west.

25. The ancient Persian religion founded by the prophet Zoroaster espoused the worship of the daily Ormazd in the context of a universal struggle between the forces of light and of darkness.

26. Mosa Javan, *Zoroaster Laws or Vandidad of Zoroaster's Holy Book,* 525 (Iran, Tehran, 1953) [In Farsi].

27. Mohammad bagher Karami, *Introduction on Criminal Justice System in Ancient Iran*, (Khate sevvom, 1380) in Farsi; Ava Vahedi, *Criminal Justice System in Sasanian Era* (Mizan Publication, 1380) [in Farsi].

28. Morteza Ravandi, *Revolution of Law and Administration of Justice* (Tehran, Iran, 1988) [In Farsi].

29. General Penal Code of Iran, Art 173 (1923) [In Farsi].

30. *Id,* Art 273.

31. Statute Regarding the Transferring of Property, Art 3 (1923) [In Farsi].

32. Abolition of flogging Statute, Single Clause (1966) [In Farsi].

33. Iraj Goldouzian, *Special Criminal Law* (Iran, Tehran: Mizan Publication, 2001) [In Farsi].

34. Islamic Penal Code of Iran, Art 729 (1991) [In Farsi].

Chapter 2

Incarceration v. Corporal Punishment

> And as long as we don't look at what happens on the inside, as long as we refuse to consider alternatives, nothing will change.[1]

PRISON OVERCROWDING CURE

Flaws of Incarceration

The father of modern criminology was Cesare Beccaria, who, in 1764, wrote a famous treatise called "On Crimes and Punishments." He pointed an accusing finger at the judges of his days because he said, their unbridled direction had led to the horrendous punishments of the eighteenth century: drawing and quartering, breaking on the wheel, and many other terrible punishments. Beccaria believed that the mind of a criminal needed to be changed and could be changed by punishing it rather than the body.[2] Unfortunately, systematic imposition of psychic punishments is impossible; mental punishment is possible only indirectly by the professional approach, so prison became the chosen alternative!

The French Philosopher Michel Foucault's work on the history of corporal punishment has been highly influential in the field of penology as well. In his 1975 book *Discipline and Punish*, Foucault argued that corporal punishment has been used as a tool of power and control throughout history and that it has been used to maintain social order and to punish those who do not conform to the norms of society. He argued that the use of corporal punishment has been to create a sense of fear and obedience in those who are subjected to it.[3]

Foucault was a major proponent of the idea that harsh punishments are not effective in deterring crime. He said that the use of harsh punishments, such as the physical punishments, only serves to further entrench the power of the state and its ability to control its citizens.[4]

Michel Foucault's views on the use of harsh punishments have been influential in the development of modern criminal justice systems. His views have been used to challenge the use of the physical punishments and to advocate for more humane forms of punishment. In *Discipline and Punish*, Foucault made the case that early modern criminal justice was focused on inflicting punishment on the body, but Bentham's Panopticon and the modern prison were designed to control the mind and soul of the incarcerated. Foucault's work leaves one with doubts that modern humane prisons are in fact more humane, even though he graphically shows the brutality of corporal punishment systems. But the majority of Americans think the contemporary US prison system is broken.

Millions of Americans find themselves confined in excessively crowded, violent, and dehumanizing prisons, devoid of effective rehabilitation programs. Despite making up close to 5% of the global population, the United States accounts for over 20% of the world's incarcerated individuals. Since 1970, the incarcerated population in the United States has increased by 500%. Currently there are 2.1 million people in jail and prison in the United States. Incarceration is expensive and the United States spends over $80 billion on incarceration each year. Another important issue of the American prison system is racial discrimination. One out of every three African American boys born today can expect to go to prison in his lifetime, as can one of every six Latino boys—compared to one of every seventeen white boys.[5] African Americans are incarcerated for drug offenses at a rate ten times greater than that of whites, even though African Americans and whites use drugs at roughly the same rates.[6]

Prison as a form of punishment has failed globally. The global prison population has been steadily increasing, with close to 11 million people behind bars around the world. Prison overcrowding is not the only flaw of the prison system, but it is a major obstacle to achieving a safe, secure, healthy, and humane prison environment, and it affects the rehabilitative purpose of punishment. Since the recognition that imprisonment alone is insufficient to meet the objectives of criminal sanctions and the uncovering of human rights violations in the prison systems, imprisonment should be considered a last resort. Therefore, the focus of the criminal justice systems should be on the use of alternatives to imprisonment.[7]

The global review of traditional model of incarceration has failed for the following reasons:

- Financial costs;
- "Schools of crime"—prisoners educate each other in criminal matters;
- Reintegration with society;
- Recidivism rate is high;
- Prison records make it difficult to get a job on release which can lead back into crime;
- Offenders' families suffer through no fault of their own;
- Failed to incorporate the rehabilitative ideals of criminal punishment.

The inability of imprisonment to efficiently achieve the goals of punishment compels us to look for an alternative to imprisonment. This lack of recognition of the value proposition of incarceration has resulted in a significant increase in questioning the use of this sanction. This apparent anomaly within the existing punishment framework calls for all the stakeholders in the prison system to recognize the enormity of this challenge and act accordingly.

On May 23, 2011, the US Supreme Court in *Brown v. Plata* upheld a court order requiring California to release up to 46,000 prisoners to solve the issue of overcrowding in the state's prisons. The wretched prison conditions cited in Justice Anthony Kennedy's majority decision make the notion of corporal punishment a bit more palatable after this case and similar cases.[8]

As the American criminal justice system has shifted away from a rehabilitative framework into a more punitive model, the time has come to consider a more effective and human alternative to incarceration. Although Islamic criminal justice systems use judicial corporal punishments as an alternative to imprisonment, a lack of recognition of human dignity in religious criminal justice systems prevents us from adopting the same judicial corporal punishments and sentencing mechanisms that extract human capital value at all levels within contemporary society.

By reviewing the experience of using judicial corporal punishments in Islamic nations and by focusing on collateral consequences of incarceration, we need to decide if reinstatement of judicial corporal punishment has any viability for the US criminal justice system.

Incarceration in Islamic Criminal Justice Systems

Incarceration as a punishment in criminal justice systems originated in Western countries only a few centuries ago, then spread to other parts of the world. Muslim jurists devoted limited attention to prison as a form of punishment, and Muslim jurists of pre-classical and classical era concentrated their attention on pre-trial and administrative detention and imprisonment for debt.

Although imprisonment existed in Islamic criminal justice systems in the second, sixth, and eighteenth centuries, the main use of imprisonment was for pre-trial detention and administrative detention, especially imprisonment for debt. Thus, punitive detention did not have the same status in premodern *Sharia* law that it does in modern Islamic criminal justice systems.[9] Even in contemporary Islamic criminal justice systems, punitive detention is an alternative enacted mainly in conjunction with corporal punishments under *hudud*[10] *or taazir*[11] (for more information regarding categories of crime and punishments in Islamic criminal justice systems, refer to chapter 5). For example, several theft crimes are punishable by flogging or imprisonment (for more information, refer to chapter 5).

Neither the Quran nor the *sunnah* (tradition of Prophet Mohammad) provided any reference to prison as a form of punishment, and it seems safe to conclude that incarceration as a form of punishment did not have the same status in classical *Sharia* law that it does in current Islamic criminal justice systems. In Islamic jurisprudence, imprisonment mainly applied to minor discretionary punishments (*taazir*) for a period of less than a year. In contemporary Islamic criminal justice systems, incarceration for the long term is reserved for the worst of the worst and dangerous criminals.[12] Under Islamic criminal justice systems, prison is often considered more severe compared to corporal punishment.[13]

Even some contemporary Islamic jurists believe in abolition of prison. One example is Jāved Aḥmad Ghāmidī,[14] a Pakistani religious scholar and jurist. His most significant critique of the carceral system came in an article called *Prison as Punishment*, which was published in July 1989.[15] In his other publication *Hudūd and Discretionary Punishment: A Few Important Points*, he has criticized and strongly rejected incarceration as a form of punishment.[16] Ghāmidī's article was written under a backdrop of the Islamization of the Pakistan criminal justice system and Islamic reforms to Pakistan's legal system. A *Hudūd* Ordinance had been introduced in 1979, and by 1990 an ordinance on Qiṣāṣ and Diyat was also introduced to the Pakistan criminal justice system.

After the Islamization of criminal law in 1970s, more Islamic countries shifted from a secular criminal justice system to an Islamic criminal justice system. Therefore, the use of judicial corporal punishment increased in these countries, and less attention was on incarceration. Although imprisonment was still one of the main form of punishments in contemporary Islamic criminal justice systems, it's mainly available as an alternative to flogging. The number of crimes punishable by incarceration has decreased compared to the pre-Islamization of laws in Islamic nations.

Historically, the question of the separation of religion and state has long been one of the central battles of liberalization and state formation, especially in the Middle East. This was in part because, unlike other identity categories or sources of affiliation, religion made competing demands of obedience on the individuals constituting the state. In some Islamic nations, religion is also a competing source of law, and it's above the law. Elsewhere, there is a long history of intervention by political parties that structure legal systems.

These characteristics of religion continue to have important implications in the contemporary criminal justice systems of Muslim nations. The rejection of Western domination and the rise of Islamization of criminal law in 1970s gave birth to Islamic criminal justice systems inspired by *Sharia* law. In these nations, there is a conflict between the notion of rule of law and religion, and the Islamization of penal codes changed the meaning of the rule of law.

Another example of Islamization of criminal law was in Iran. After the Islamic Revolution in 1979, the secular criminal justice system was replaced by an Islamic criminal justice system with more concentration on corporal punishments compared to incarceration. Although imprisonment is one of the main forms of punishments in the Islamic criminal justice system of Iran, several crimes are now punishable by corporal punishments.

Although in Islamic criminal justice systems judicial corporal punishments are considered as a primary alternative to imprisonment, traditional noncustodial punishments such as parole, fine, and probation are a part of Iranian criminal justice and have been used as well. The use of alternatives to incarceration or noncustodial measures is a major part of the United Nations Office on Drugs and Crime's integrated and multidisciplinary approach to prison reform, which takes full account of the need to relate prison reform to broader criminal justice reform. It is also an area that witnessed significant developments at the national level, with the entry of the new Iranian Penal Code, which includes a chapter on alternatives to imprisonment (Chapter 9) in April 2013 and the issue of important instructions by the head of the judiciary for "criminal depopulation of prisons" in May 2013.[17]

The recent Islamic Penal Code of Iran has expanded the use of alternatives to imprisonment. According to Article 66 of the new Iranian Penal Code, if the prisoner has been sentenced to ninety-one days to six months imprisonment, the alternative to imprisonment will be imposed. Although traditional noncustodial punishments such as parole, fines, and probation have been a part of the Iranian criminal justice system for a long time, the use of these alternatives has been expanded, and nontraditional alternatives such as daily fines, supervised probation, home confinement, and community service have been added to the Iranian corrections system.

THE THEATER OF PUNISHMENT

Pro-Corporal Punishment Scholars in Western World

Because incarceration is both expensive and ineffective, a number of Western scholars believe judicial corporal punishment is an appropriate alternative to imprisonment. Although the pro-corporal punishment faction is a minority view in criminology, it is a louder and more vocal group in recent decades, strengthened by a sense that many US prisons have extremely bad conditions. Pro-judicial corporal punishment scholars believe if incarceration is a justifiable method of punishment, then so is this type of judicial corporal punishment. A minority of contemporary academics defend certain types of corporal punishment such as whipping, electric shock, temporary organ failure, and e-carceration.

Among criminologists, Graeme Newman defends judicial corporal punishment by appeal to a retributive theory of punishment. He is a distinguished professor emeritus at the School of Criminal Justice, University of Albany. Newman in his book *Just and Painful: A Case for The Corporal Punishment of Criminals* presents a reactionary alternative to the high cost "schools of crime" we call prisons. He advocates punishment that fits the crime,[18] stating that "all crimes—whether violent or property crimes—could best be served retributively by various kinds of violent punishments."[19] Newman concludes that judicial corporal punishment "can meet with the philosophical challenge of just punishment and . . . can also go much of the way to solving the fiscal problem of criminal punishment."[20]

Another defender of judicial corporal punishment is Peter Moskos. He is an American professor at John Jay College of Criminal Justice. Peter Moskos makes the case that convicts should be given the option to choose corporal punishment as an alternative to incarceration. Peter Moskos poses a simple question: Given the choice between prison and whipping, he believes incarceration is long, torturous, and psychologically destructive, whereas flogging is a short burst of searing pain. "By giving offenders the option of exchanging time behind bars for the lash, we can punish criminals, save money, spare families, and ensure that justice is served."[21]

Moskos writes that both republicans and democrats should approve flogging as a substitute for prison.

> If you're a conservative, flogging holds appeal as efficient, cheap, and old-fashioned punishment for wrongdoing . . . it's a get-tough approach . . . and nothing is tougher than the lash. If you're a liberal and your goal is to punish more humanely, then you must accept that the present system is an inhumane failure.[22]

Peter Moskos' main reasoning is in response to the broken American prison system. He defends flogging to start an honest discussion on punishment and alternatives to prison. Moskos claims "we need to find a new way to punish, an option that won't subject offenders and society to this expensive and immoral failure. If flogging is that option, well, then bring on the lash."[23]

If we accept Moskos' idea as a serious option for incarceration, it could have profound consequences for a nation that incarcerates its citizens at a rate that's higher than the other countries. Clearly, we have to find a way to reduce prison populations, and this just might be a logical one.[24]

Among philosophers, Geoffrey Scarre defends judicial corporal punishment on utilitarian[25] grounds. He argues corporal punishment is not inevitably crueler or more demanding than conventionally proffered punitive methods and that consideration should be given to its limited experimental reintroduction.[26] Ole Martin Moen is another pro-judicial corporal punishment philosopher. Moen is a Norwegian philosopher at Oslo Metropolitan University. He believes:

> Incarceration, which is today's norm, also involves violence (albeit less visibly compared to judicial corporal punishment), and we know for certain that it has lasting negative effects on the mental health of convicts. On the other hand, caning has several beneficial features: it costs less; it punishes only the convicts; it

> does not destroy the social and economic networks that many convicts depend upon to reintegrate into society after release; it does not cause convicts to socialize with other convicts over long stretches of time; it makes it harder for us to evade what we are doing when we punish; and it arguably gives us a greater deterrent effect in return for each unit of harm that we inflict.[27]

Another defender of judicial corporal punishment is John Gleissner. He is an author and lawyer. He has graduated from Auburn University and Vanderbilt Law School. Since 1977, he has been practicing law in Alabama. He believes:

> The effectiveness and efficiency of JCP in deterring crime, allowing rehabilitation, and achieving visible retribution will eventually decide its fate in the U.S. as an additional punishment option. Only the passage of JCP legislation for a period of time sufficient to establish its benefits and disadvantages in our society fairly tests this mode of punishment in light of scientific advancements and social developments during its disuse. With the enormous challenges and limitations associated with all other forms of punishment, a jurist could not easily bar a traditional weapon in the fight against crime, prison overcrowding, massive incarceration, and now intractable pain.[28]

Gleissner hopes originalists on the Supreme Court would uphold judicial corporal punishment legislation.

Senator Tom Cotton is another proponent of more punitive criminal justice system. Senator Cotton hopes for low-level and nonviolent offenders. He believes: "the criminal justice system in the United States is extraordinarily lenient. In fact, it is more lenient than at any point in our history."[29]

Although a number of Western scholars are pro-judicial corporal punishment, their claims are not based on scientific studies, and they have not referred to any empirical study on the current use of judicial corporal punishments to conclude if the reinstatement of these punishments is effective. For counter arguments regarding this section, please refer to chapter 3.

Prison as a Form of Cruel and Unusual Punishment

Punishment by imprisonment is not per se cruel and unusual; it may be offensive when the duration of a sentence is so excessive or disproportionate to the crime committed as to shock the conscience and reason of people generally.

In determining what punishments should be regarded as incompatible with human rights standards, the result has been that in many societies long periods of imprisonment, sometimes but not always or necessarily for life, have emerged as the ultimate penalty for the most serious offenses.

Anti-cruel and unusual principles have also played a part in deciding how imprisonment must be implemented to meet the requirements of international human rights law. One insight is that it requires the imposition and implementation of punishment, including imprisonment, to be viewed holistically.[30] Thus, for example, the International Covenant on Civil and Political Rights contains mutually reinforcing provisions. The prohibition on cruel, inhuman, or degrading punishment in Article 7 and on servitude and forced or compulsory labor in Article 8, combined with a further prohibition on the loss of liberty without due legal process in Article 9.[31]

Further development of international human rights standards relating to prisons may eventually be achieved through the implementation of an optional protocol to the International Convention against Torture and Other Cruel, Inhuman, and Degrading Treatment or Punishment.[32] The Optional Protocol provides for the establishment of a regular system of visits by independent international bodies to all places where persons who are deprived of their liberty are detained.[33] Inevitably the proposed Subcommittee on Prevention, which will be responsible for such inspections, will have to develop guidelines for what is to be regarded as torture and as cruel, inhuman, or degrading punishment or treatment. In doing so it is bound to draw on existing international standards.

These issues emerging as international standards become even greater when one considers that a similar process of standard setting is underway at the regional level. In Europe this is most prominent. The European Court of Human Rights, by interpreting the prohibition on inhuman or degrading treatment or punishment in Article 3 of the European Convention on Human Rights, has somewhat haltingly developed its own standards for the imposition[34] and implementation of punishment, as well as for imprisonment generally.[35] The 1987 European Prison Rules and other recommendations of the Council of Europe on punishment and prisons have bolstered this process.[36]

Cruel and unusual punishment is aimed primarily at the kind of punishment imposed, not its duration. Nevertheless, where the duration of a sentence imposed on one convicted of crime is so disproportionate to the offense committed as to shock the moral sense of the community, the punishment is prohibited.[37] In determining whether the length of a sentence offends a prohibition against cruel and unusual punishment, the courts will look to such matters as the nature of the offense, the character of the offender, the penalties imposed in the jurisdiction for other offenses, and the penalties imposed in other jurisdictions for the same offense.[38] Therefore increased sentence statutes, multiple sentence in single prosecution, indeterminate sentences, and unequal sentences for codefendants are successful challenges to imprisonment that to some may appear disproportionately harsh.

Statutes imposing *life imprisonment upon habitual criminals*[39] have been challenged as cruel and unusual punishment on several grounds. They should not inflict double jeopardy,[40] violate ex post facto[41] clauses, or deny equal protection of law,[42] except where such punishment is disproportionate to the gravity of the prior crimes alleged and proved.[43]

Life sentence without possibility of parole does not per se constitute a cruel and unusual punishment. In United States, statutes prescribing life sentences without possibility of parole have been upheld in cases involving murder,[44] kidnapping,[45] bank robbery,[46] drug or narcotic offenses,[47] and aggravated rape.[48] Although regarding juveniles,[49] a statute providing a penalty of life imprisonment without benefit of parole for the offense of rape has been held to constitute cruel and unusual punishment.[50]

The idea of *indeterminate sentences* was to individualize punishment to better fit the needs of prisoners and society. Indeterminate sentences are of four types: (1) Most provide for minimum and maximum limits. (2) Set the minimum but allow the judge or jury to establish the maximum. (3) Set the maximum but allow the judge or jury to set the minimum. (4) Authorize the judge or jury to fix either minimum or maximum.[51] There are several objections to these sentences because they permit an unlawful delegation of judicial power to an administrative body, they interfere with the pardoning power of the executive, they violate the separation of powers doctrine, and they are void for uncertainty;[52] therefore, they inflict cruel and unusual punishment.

There are three possibilities when the defendant participating in a single activity may be sentenced to *multiple terms of imprisonment*: 1. When the statute separates each step in a given process.[53] 2. Unrelated statutes may overlap and allow multiple sentences that a single act may result in conviction on several counts.[54] 3. A defendant may be sentenced to multiple terms of imprisonment because of a single act, when more than one victim is involved.[55]

The last challenge to imprisonment as an excessive punishment is *unequal sentences for codefendants*. Disparate sentences are often imposed on codefendants charged with the same offense. In some cases, the most obvious disparities result when the trials are separated. Although sometimes we cannot consider unequal sentences for codefendants as a violation of cruel and unusual, generally because the facts of the case justify the disparity or that the sentence was well within statutory limits.[56]

By considering the nature of the offense, the character of the offender, the penalties imposed in the jurisdiction for other offenses, and the penalties imposed in other jurisdictions for the same offense, the difficulty is asserting the gravity of offense comparing similarly grave offense and comparing the offense in different jurisdictions.

Of course, some offenses involving violent harm to human beings will always and anywhere be regarded as serious, but the problem is what else should be regarded to be as serious as these offenses or to be more serious than some of them.[57] It is easy to prove a mandatory sentence of life imprisonment for a minimum of thirty years as applied to a fifteen-year-old child convicted of murder after standing trial as an adult is neither cruel nor unusual punishment within the meaning of this prohibition but three years for conviction of adultery under Idaho Code[58] constitutes cruel and unusual punishment. But would it be grossly excessive to provide life imprisonment for mere possession of a certain amount of drugs? Moreover, what if the possible dissemination of drugs can be so grave as to impose life imprisonment?

The second difficulty is there is no subjective standard of gravity for judges to compare. Sometimes two offenses that are judicially determined to be similarly grave receive dissimilar penalties. We cannot say a harsher penalty is cruel and unusual because similarly the grave crimes would not necessarily be comparable since there are other justifications such as deterrent or rehabilitation effects to consider. Deterrent is not only depending on the amount of penalty but also upon its certainty. Crimes that are less grave but more difficult to detect may warrant higher punishment or grave crimes of that sort that are committed once in lifetime by law-abiding citizens will profit from rehabilitation.[59]

The final difficulty is comparing the offense from jurisdiction to jurisdiction. In a federal system, some states will always bear the distinction of treating particular offenders more severely than other states or a state may criminalize an act that other states do not criminalize at all. The different needs and concerns of other states may induce them to treat possession of 672 grams of cocaine as a relatively minor offense.

The legislature, and likewise a city council under a delegated authority, may prescribe definite terms of imprisonment for crimes or violations of statutes or city ordinances without depriving the judiciary of discretionary power to fix reasonable limits, so long as the rights of citizens have not been violated a sentence within the limits of a statute cannot be said to be cruel and inhuman.

NOTES

1. Peter Moskos, *In Defense of Flogging*, 5 (Basic Books, 2011).

2. Cesare Beccaria, On Crimes and Punishments, for a look at what is perhaps the first published opinion regarding the use of mental rather than physical punishment in a modernizing society. Note that Beccaria did arguably support corporal punishment at an early point in his career, but he shifted to a belief that imprisonment for life, with hard labor, was the best punishment available to civilized man.

3. Michel Foucault, *Discipline and Punish: The Birth of Prison*, New York: Vintage Books (1975).

4. *Id.*

5. See Mass Incarceration: The Whole Pie 2023, https://www.prisonpolicy.org/reports/pie2023.html.

6. *Id.*

7. See Alternatives to Imprisonment, https://www.unodc.org/unodc/en/justice-and-prison-reform/cpcj-alternatives-to-imprisonment.html.

8. Mansfield Frazier, California Prisons are Overcrowded? Is Flogging Answer, *The Daily Beast*, July 2017.

9. Irene Schneider, Imprisonment in Pre-Classical and Classical Islamic Law, *Islamic Law Society* 2, no. 2, 157–173 (1995).

10. Under *had* or *hudud*, important crimes deemed to threaten the existence of Islam are punishable by penalties set by the Quran, or by the *Sunnah* or *Sunna* (tradition of Prophet Mohammad). Islamic jurists consider these sanctions immutable. They conclude that the judge is left with no discretion.

11. Public authorities set their own punishment, and the judge has wide discretion.

12. Cherif Bassiouni & Gamal Badr, The Shariah: Sources, Interpretation and Rule-Making, 1 *UCLA J. Islamic & Near E. L.* 135, 150 (2002).

13. *Id*, at 232, 233.

14. Ghāmidī was born to a Sufi family in the Panjab, Pakistan. His early education included secular schools, Arabic, and Persian He then studied philosophy, English literature and Islamic studies at Government College in Lahore. He actively studied under his most influential teacher Amīn Aḥsan Iṣlaḥī (1904–1997).

15. Javad Ahmad Ghamadi, Oayad ki Saza (Prison as Punishment), *Ishraq*, no. 11, 37–42 (July 1989).

16. Javad Ahmad Ghamadi, *Hudud and Discretionary Punishment: A Few Important Points*, in Burhan (Proof), 7th ed. 143–146 (Lahore: al-Mawrid, 2009).

17. Alasti, Sanaz Alasti, and Eric Bronson, " Corrections in Iran" *The Encyclopedia of Corrections* (2017): 1–5.

18. Graeme Newman, *Just and Painful: A Case for the Corporal Punishment of-Criminals*, 114 (Macmillan Publishing Company, 1983); Moskos, supra note 1, at 21.

19. *Id,* at 25.

20. *Id*, at 5.

21. Peter Moskos, *supra* note 1, 153–154

22. *Id.*

23. *Id.*

24. The doctrine that an action is right insofar as it promotes happiness and that the greatest happiness of the greatest number should be the guiding principle of conduct.

25. Geoffrey Scarre, *Corporal Punishment*, Ethical Theory and Moral Practice 6, no. 3, 295–316 (2003).

26. Ole Martin Moen, *Judicial Corporal Punishment*, J. Ethics & Soc. Phil., 17, 27 (2020).

27. John Dewar Gleissner, *Prison Overcrowding Cure: Judicial Corporal Punishment of Adults*, Criminal Law Bulletin 49, no. 4, 2 (2013).

28. Barry Latzer, *Myth of Over punishment: A Defense of the American Justice System and a Proposal to Reduce Incarceration While Protecting the Public* (Republic Book Publishing, 2022).

29. *Mbenge v Zaire*, Communication No. 16/1977 (25 Mar 1983), UN Doc CCPR/C/OP/2 at 76 (1990).

30. Also see Rule 71(1) of the United Nations Standard Minimum Rules for the Treatment of Prisoners.

31. GA Res 39/46, 10 Dec 1984, 39 UN GAOR Supp (No 51) 197, UN Doc E/CN 4/1984/72.

32. GA Res A/Res/57/199, 18 Dec 2002.

33. B Emmerson, A. Ashworth, *Human Rights and Criminal Justice*, 479–514 (Sweet & Maxwell, London, 2001).

34. *Peers v Greece* (2001) 33 EHRR 1192.

35. Recommendation R (87)3 of the Committee of Ministers of the Council of Europe and Recommendation R (82) 16 of the Committee of Ministers of the Council of Europe on Prison Leave.

36. 21A Am Jur 2d Criminal Law § 973.

37. *Id.*

38. Habitual offender statutes, variously known as increased sentence statutes, enhanced punishment statutes, recidivist statute, and multiple offender statutes.

39. Double jeopardy prohibits anyone from being prosecuted twice for substantially the same crime.

40. Ex post facto is most typically used to refer to a criminal statute that punishes actions retroactively, thereby criminalizing conduct that was legal when originally performed.

41. See Graham v. West Virginia, 224 U.S. 616 (1912), McDonald v. Massachusetts, 180 U.S. 311 (1901), and Moore v. Missouri, 159 U.S. 673 (1895).

42. 21A Am Jur 2d Criminal Law § 974.

43. State v. Farrow, 118 N.H. 296, 386 A.2d 808 (1978).

44. Beard v. State, 262 Ind. 643, 323 N.E.2d 216 (1975).

45. People v. Ferguson, 60 Mich. App. 302, 230 N.W.2d 406 (1975).

46. State v. Stetson, 317 So. 2d 172 (La. 1975).

47. State v. Iaukea, 56 Haw. 343, 537 P.2d 724 (1975).

48. Workman v. Com., 429 S.W.2d 374, 33 A.L.R.3d 326 (Ky. 1968).

49. Miller v. Alabama (2012), in this case Supreme Court held that mandatory sentences of life without the possibility of parole are unconstitutional for juvenile offenders.

50. "*Indeterminate Sentence Law*" Harvard Law Review 50 (winter 1937).

51. *Id.*

52. For instance, when prosecution of counterfeiting allows for prosecution for possessing plates, concealing, manufacturing, and possessing counterfeit money as well as buying, selling, exchanging, transferring, receiving, delivering or passing counterfeit money.

53. For instance, when an Act allows prosecution for the purchase, sale, distribution, exchange, or gift of narcotics, also prohibits the purchase, sale or concealment of illegally imported drugs as well as the importation itself.

54. See 18 U.S.C. secs. 471–74, 21 U.S.C. sec, 173 (1952), also Islamic Penal Code of Iran, Art 46-7 (1997).

55. Howard Alperin, *Length of Sentence as Violation of Constitutional Provisions Prohibiting Cruel and Unusual Punishment*, 33 ALR3d.

56. Kristin O'Donnell Tubb, *Freedom from Cruel and Unusual Punishment*, 106–108 (Greenhaven press, 2005).

57. Idaho code, secs 18-6601.

58. Kristin O'Donnell Tubb, supra note 56, at 108–109.

59. *Id.*

Chapter 3

Penological Objectives and Advantages of Corporal Punishment

All people feel pain as pain, and only [t]he ways they react to this pain may vary.[1]

PENOLOGICAL OBJECTIVES

Will Corporal Punishment Deter Crime?

As to the supporting by legitimate penological purposes, rehabilitation, deterrence, incapacitation, and retribution are legitimate penological objectives. Whipping could potentially serve retribution, rehabilitation, temporary incapacitation, and deterrence objectives; however, the evidence concerning whether whipping is an effective form of specific deterrence is inconclusive. Although the experts may disagree as to the value of corporal punishment in deterring crime, the same debate exists regarding imprisonment and other forms of popular punishment. It is reasonable to believe that whipping will be as successful in preventing crime as imprisonment. Intuitively, however, it is easy to believe that whipping could serve as an effective general deterrent. Although rehabilitation and deterrence are the most popular penal objectives today, a punishment is also valid if it is an effective form of retribution. Undoubtedly, whipping can satisfy retribution objectives.[2]

Only three substantial studies on judicial corporal punishment in criminal justice have been conducted. These studies have been conducted in Delaware, England, and Iran. The Delaware study was conducted by Professor Robert Caldwell in 1947 and published in his interesting book *Red Hannah: Delaware Whipping Post.* As I mentioned earlier, Delaware was the last state in the United States to abolish whipping as a criminal punishment. Professor Caldwell compared the rate of the recommittal of (1) those criminals sentenced to whipping and who were not whipped with (2) those criminals who were sentenced to whipping and who were whipped. Based on his findings, Caldwell concluded that whipping should be abolished.[3]

The British research into whipping displayed a similar bias. The report of the committee on corporal punishment was published by the Home Office in March 1938. Its conclusion was: "We are not satisfied that corporal punishment has that exceptionally effective influence as a deterrent which is usually claimed for it by those who advocate its use as a penalty."[4] Social scientists' conclusions were invariable that corporal punishment should be abolished because it could not be demonstrated to have a deterrent effect.[5]

An Iranian study compares the number of crimes punishable by flogging in the 1980s with the 1990s. In 1984, a discretionary punishment statute was ratified in Iran. Under this statute, flogging was considered as a punishment for sixty-four different crimes, but in 1997 chapter five of Islamic Penal Code was ratified, and it replaced the discretionary punishment statute of 1984. This statute also includes flogging for different crimes, but the incidence of flogging decreased compared to the 1984 statute.[6] Based on the new statute, the number of crimes punishable by flogging was reduced to thirty-five, and flogging was substituted by imprisonment (please see figure 3.1).

The crimes punishable by flogging are mainly crimes against property and theft crimes in the Islamic criminal justice system of Iran. If flogging is a deterrent, the number of theft crimes should increase after the enactment of a new statute in 1997 and using imprisonment instead of flogging. The

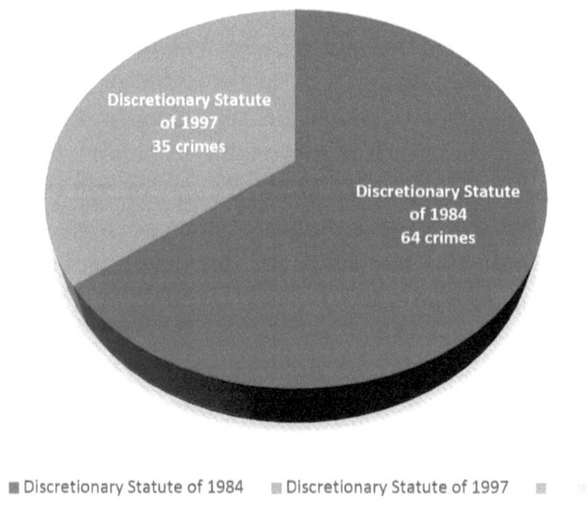

Figure 3.1 Frequency of Flogging as a Discretionary Punishment in Islamic Penal Code (1997) Compared to Discretionary Statute (1984). *Source*: Figure created by author.

researchers surveyed a thirteen-year period of theft crimes in Iran and found a counter-deterrent or brutalizing effect of flogging. Since theft crimes have decreased dramatically after the new statute, corporal punishment may cause more crimes rather than deter them. The study concluded that there is no consistent evidence that shifting from flogging to incarceration increases crime, and corporal punishment is a greater deterrent compared to incarceration.[7]

Legislation enacting the punishment of whipping must be artfully drawn. Legislation providing for whipping that is intended to cause pain in excess of what is necessary to achieve the desired deterrence is unlawful. Accordingly, many of the early whippings in US history would not be permissible today. For example, in 1715 Maryland adulterers were fined money and tobacco and were "whipped upon his or their bare bodies till the blood do appear, so many stripes (not exceeding thirty-nine) as the justices before whom such conviction shall be, shall adjudge." Similarly, canings, such as those administered to Michael Fay (for more information, refer to chapter 5) would not meet Eighth Amendment standards because they often draw blood and cause offenders to lose consciousness.[8]

Although the effectiveness of whipping as a specific deterrent is unclear and additional research is necessary, it would be reasonable for a legislature to determine that retribution and general deterrence would be served. The fact that whipping is used in both the American home and school can be relied upon by a legislature as evidence of its value. The apparent success of whipping as a deterrent in other nations can also be used. Of course, criminal offenders are different than children, and the cultural differences between nations may make these analogies faulty. But the constitutional inquiry is limited to determining whether the decision to whip was made recklessly or maliciously. If, after whipping has been tried and tested, the penological data evinces that it is not successful in achieving any one of the recognized penological objectives, then the continuation of the punishment would be unnecessary. Accordingly, it is necessary to examine the punishment objectives that whipping may achieve.

Retribution as a Valid Objective for Corporal Punishment

As previously stated, retribution is a valid objective. In *Gregg v. Georgia,*[9] the court recognized retribution as a sound penological objective, and in *Spaziano v. Florida,*[10] the court stated that "retribution is an element of all punishments society imposes." But what is retribution? Retribution can be troublesome because it has vengeance at its core. It can be defined as "a disguised form of vengeance." Not all commentators assume that vengeance is bad. James F. Stephen claimed that the criminal law stands to the passion of revenge in much the same relation as marriage to sexual appetite.[11] Stephen assumed that by channeling vengeance through an organized justice system, unruly violence, which can be highly destructive, will be thwarted.[12] In this sense, the retribution rationale is validated. But what if society's passions are heightened due to a particularly heinous crime? Could the punishments intended to be prohibited by the cruel and unusual definition be practiced? Yes. Therefore, defining retribution as satisfying the public's need for revenge is not adequate. It may play a part, but it is not sufficiently limiting.

The nature of the crime and the resulting injuries and damages to individuals and the public will also be factors in determining the limits of retributive punishment. In *Tison v. Arizona,*[13] the court held that "the heart of the retribution rationale is that a criminal sentence must be directly related to the personal culpability of the criminal offender." True, this standard is vague, and the determination of whether a sentence serves rehabilitation, incapacitation, or deterrence objectives is more precise. But few punishments will be based solely on retribution, and, when one is, the *Tison* standard provides courts with the discretion necessary to prevent cruelty. It is a safety net.

What more can retribution be? In previous times, punishment was thought to be for the benefit of the offender. It had religious significance and a secular purpose. Offenders paid their debt to society. David Starkweather noted that "criminal behavior constitute[s] a violation of the moral or natural order . . . and, having offended that order, require[s] payment of some kind." Therefore, a criminal is punished because he or she deserves it.[14] This justification for punishment is appropriately called the principle of "just deserts." In the theory of "just deserts," both the offender and society benefit from the punishment. This latter objective is the one most thought of today—just deserts. So, maybe the limit of retributive justice is the amount of punishment necessary for an offender to make amends.

Corporal Punishment and Optimal Incapacitation

Imprisonment as an incapacitative sanction may entail social costs that are not present with corporal punishment. This argument is based on two assumptions. First, some crimes may involve an undeterrable organ—that is, the undeterred bodily means to affecting a crime—only. Second, some corporal punishment may be used to incapacitate the particular organ temporarily.

As is widely known, corporal punishment has had a much longer history than imprisonment. Indeed, "eye for eye, tooth for tooth, hand for hand, foot for foot"[15] has been a familiar theme in Jewish, Christian, and Muslim societies. Various types of corporal punishment—such as hand amputation, blinding, or other forms of organ retaliation, and branding—represented the most severe forms of corporal punishment. Whipping, caning, castration, and dismembering of limbs were less damaging corporal punishments. We have to know why these corporal punishments, relative to imprisonment, are no longer popular—their social costs increased as civilization further developed. Capital punishment was not exercised for all crimes; instead, flogging and mutilation were adopted for some. Why? The old retributive theory or the modern economic theory of marginal deterrence can provide an answer; however, incapacitation as an alternative explanation will be emphasized here.[16]

Capital punishment and castration were alternatives used to stop adultery and rape, and a rational wealth-maximizing emperor would refrain from capital punishment so that the offender could still work and pay taxes. Thus, optimal incapacitation implies that both adulterers and rapists should be castrated but not beheaded. After castration was abolished in China, capital punishment was used to punish those who were convicted for the more serious cases of adultery and rape. In contrast, after the abolition of mutilation in 167 BC, convicts who originally would have been mutilated were punished by flogging. Frequently, convicts received so many strokes that they were in effect beaten to death. As a result, many people, including informed intellectuals, considered both changes in criminal punishment (the abolition of castration and mutilation) to be cruel.

Therefore, some scholars found that imprisonment is not optimal and that corporal punishment—for example, whipping, caning, castration, and other forms of punishment—can be optimal incapacitative measures against certain undeterrable criminal acts. The temporary incapacitation of the particular organ at fault would incur less social cost, compared to imprisonment or mutilation. With recent advances in biological, medical, and other technologies, it is not impossible to develop new ways to temporarily incapacitate some organs by way of injection or electric shock without creating long-term side effects (please see table 3.1).

Table 3.1 An Extended Structure of Optimal Incapacitation

Punishment	Duration of the Propensity to Commit an Offense	Extent of Bodily Involvement
Capital Punishment	Permanent	Whole Body
Life Imprisonment without Possibility of Parole	Permanent	Whole Body
Amputation of Body	Permanent	Organ
Castration	Permanent	Organ
Term Imprisonment	Temporary	Whole Body
Whipping	Temporary	Organ
Shame Punishments	Temporary	Whole Body
E-Carceration	Temporary	Whole Body

Source: Steven S. Kan, Corporal Punishments and Optimal Incapacitation, 25 J. Legal Stud. 121 (January, 1996).

A new book by Professor Barry Latzer *The Myth of Overpunishment: A Defense of the American Justice System and a Proposal to Reduce Incarceration While Protecting the Public* proposes a new incapacitative alternative to mass incarceration and corporal punishment. He believes the expansion of electronic monitoring of convicts is the best solution of contemporary penal systems. Latzer explains how dramatically expanding the electronic monitoring capacity is a much better idea than incarceration or releasing dangerous offenders.[17]

In sum, by using a utilitarian analysis of corporal punishment, I concluded that a reform of criminal punishment need not revert to bloody corporal punishment, without consideration of rehabilitation goals. Instead, retribution, deterrence, incapacitation, and rehabilitation are all legitimate objectives, and adoption of any one penological theory is not possible. Also, if the objective of a punishment is only to inflict pain or to rob the offender of his humanity, the punishment is improper per se because it is not founded upon a sound penological purpose.

ADVANTAGES AND DISADVANTAGES OF CORPORAL PUNISHMENT

Can Corporal Punishment Be Adminstrated Without Humiliating the Offender?

Most certainly corporal punishment can be administrated without humiliating the offender. Because corporal punishment has been used for centuries in many countries as an aid to, or a replacement for, imprisonment by using it here, we could save money that is spent on prisons to achieve other social goals. By making the punishment public, we can add general and specific deterrent effects to the retributive effects already established. And by coupling the corporal punishment and shaming[18] to successfully reintegrate the offender into society.

Whitney Wiedeman who is the defender of judicial corporal punishment believes that return to judicial corporal punishments

> will strengthen the long-term specific deterrent effect on the individual and, eventually, the general deterrent effect on society as a whole. Corporal punishment would return the criminal justice system to its proper place as a small part of the system to promote the general welfare. And not only could we begin to combat the crime problem of today, but we could also see a profound reduction in youthful offenders and a greater impact on the generations to follow.[19]

Therefore, the infliction of violent punishment upon violent offenders was entirely defensible from the point of view of the ethics of retributive justice.

While the infliction of economic punishments for economic crimes is the logical punishment from the point of view of retribution, for a number of practical and moral reasons this is not defensible and that violent punishments are the most sensible solution.

Financial Costs of Corporal Punishment

The proponents of judicial corporal punishments believe it's less costly compared to imprisonment, and it could help significantly reduce the huge economic and social costs which incarceration levies on American society. Mohamed Arafa, professor of criminal justice at Alexandria University in Egypt, claims "judicial corporal punishment as implemented in Islamic criminal law meets the penal purposes of rehabilitation and deterrence more effectively."[20] Arafa believes:

> Judicial corporal punishment shifts the cost away from the taxpayers and onto the families of offenders. That is, instead of extracting dollars out of the taxpayer's pocket for vocational training programs, educational classes, counseling, and religious resources for the betterment of the criminal, the family of the criminal becomes responsible for providing these resources. And, as to the penal purpose of deterrence, the taxpayer cost of administering justice via judicial corporal punishment as implemented in Islamic criminal law is essentially limited to the price of the weapon and the wage of the punisher.[21]

While the exact cost of judicial corporal punishments has not been determined, it is much less time-consuming and therefore also much less labor and capital-intensive. Of course, cost is not all that matters in selecting a type of punishment, but insofar as the resources that are currently spent on incarceration could have been spent on rehabilitation, compensation to victims, or improved conditions in prisons for convicts who must still be incarcerated.[22]

When Is Whipping Appropriate?

For what crimes and for what offenders is whipping appropriate? Proportionality analysis is fact sensitive. The nature of a crime, the penological objectives underlying its punishment, and the particular facts of each case will determine whether a punishment is too severe. Therefore, it is not possible to draw generalized conclusions concerning the applicability of whipping under proportionality analysis. Consider the long-standing history of whipping in the United States, while in Iran it continued well into the twenty-first century. Presumably, evidence of jurisdictions that have considered, or are considering, whipping as a form of punishment would be weighted. Otherwise, no jurisdiction could ever become the first of possibly many adopting jurisdictions.

We can conclude that disproportionality of punishment is a major flaw in Iran's criminal justice system. Otherwise, this issue is arguable because flogging is not inherently cruel and inhumane. If properly regulated and proportionately imposed, flogging is equally as valid as paddling or capital punishment. Iran can begin to conform to international human rights standards without abolishing flogging. Although flogging is a disproportionate penalty for property crimes such as vandalism and drug possession, it is probably proportionate for crimes against the person, including assault, rape, and domestic violence. One of most significant problems with flogging is that it is disproportionate punishment for property crimes. By restricting flogging to violent crimes against the person, Iran[23] will retain this traditional punishment without further alienating the international community. International standards prohibit torture and ill-treatment; domestic law cannot consider whipping appropriate even for applying flogging in crimes against the person.

Pain Infliction

Throughout history, pain has proven to be important to medicine, philosophy, and religion. Without pain, pleasure would be unknown. Without pain, some forms of punishment would be ineffective. The total elimination of pain from punishment is wrong, or at least, unwise. On the other hand, unnecessary pain is also wrong. Pain inflicted for sadistic purposes or to achieve an improper objective (e.g., obtaining a confession) is wrong. The Framers had such matters in mind when they ratified the Fifth, Eighth, and Fourteenth Amendments. Of course, drawing the line between permissible and impermissible pain is the challenge. In the context of criminal justice, the infliction of pain is valid when used to achieve a legitimate purpose.

The recognition of mental and emotional pain is also important to this inquiry. It is generally accepted that the emotional and psychological needs of inmates are protected by the Eighth Amendment. Justice Brennan[24] stated that pain is not the only reason primitive punishments, such as the rack, thumbscrew, and stretching of limbs, are violative of the Eighth Amendment. He asserted that "the true significance of these punishments is that they treat members of the human race as nonhumans." The decision in *Trop v. Dulles* stands for the proposition that cruelty can transcend corporeal interests. The court held that denationalization for the crime of desertion amounts to the "total destruction of the individual's status in organized society. It is a form of punishment more primitive than torture, for it destroys for the individual the political existence that was centuries in the development."[25] Whipping does not transgress these limits. Although it does rely on pain and, to some extent, humiliation to achieve its objectives, it does not destroy a person's status in society. Nor does it serve only to satisfy sadistic desires. Moreover, in some cases, it may be more humane and penologically sound than other generally accepted forms of punishment, such as imprisonment.[26]

Considering the above hypothesis, it appears that a number of punishments still utilized today are extremely suspect. Whipping and mutilation are obvious candidates for extinction. But will all scholars agree to rule out these penalties? Following legislative and judicial approval and the current experience of judicial corporal punishments in Islamic criminal justice systems in the next chapter show certainly not.

NOTES

1. Graeme Newman, *Just and Painful: A Case for the Corporal Punishment of Criminals*, 46 (Macmillan Publishing Company, 1983).
2. *Id.*
3. Robert G. Caldwell, *Criminology*, 451–452 (2d ed. 1965).
4. Robert G. Caldwell, *Red Hannah: Delaware's Whipping Post*, 98 (Philadelphia: University of Pennsylvania Press, 1947).
5. Graeme Newman, *supra* note 1, at 127–136.
6. Iraj Goldouzian, *Special Criminal Law* (Iran, Tehran: Mizan Publication, 2001) [In Farsi].
7. Hossein Aghaie Nia, *Special Criminal Law 1 Pamphlet* (Tehran University Law School, 2001).
8. Graeme Newman, *supra* note 1, at 127–136.
9. 424 U.S. 904, 96 S.Ct. 1095 (Mem), 47 L.Ed.2d 308, U.S.Ga., February 23, 1976 (NO. 74 6257).
10.516 U.S. 1053, 116 S.Ct. 722 (Mem), 133 L.Ed.2d 674, 64 USLW 3466, U.S.Fla., January 08, 1996 (NO. 95-6471).
11. James F Stephen, *History of the Criminal Law of England (Making of the British Legal System)* (Routledge/Thoemmes P; 1 edition, 1996).
12. *Id.*
13. 454 U.S. 960, 102 S.Ct. 499 (Mem), 70 L.Ed.2d 376, U.S., November 02, 1981 (NO. 81-5634).
14. See David A. Starkweather, *Note, The Retributive Theory of 'Just Desert and Victim Participation in Plea Bargaining,* 67 Ind. L.J. 853, 854–855 (1992).
15. Bible, Exod. 21:24.
16. Whitney Wiedeman, *Special Issue: Juvenile Justice and the Criminal Law: Comment: Don't Spare the Rod: A Proposed Return to Public, Corporal Punishment on Convicts*, 23 Am. J. Crim. L. 651(1996).
17. Barry Latzer, *Myth of Over punishment: A Defense of the American Justice System and a Proposal to Reduce Incarceration While Protecting the Public* (Republic Book Publishing, 2022).

18. It is too early to tell how effective shame punishments will be in the long run. They have already had an enormous impact on offenders throughout the nation, including those in Kansas. It will be up to the lawmakers and courts to decide whether this reemerging form of punishment will continue to have a positive impact upon American jurisprudence. For certain crimes, such as drunk driving and prostitution solicitation, shame penalties are effective as a punishment as well as a deterrent. Yearning for social accountability, Judge Poe stated, unchastized wrongdoing and country club prisons, complete with color televisions and weight rooms, have left us a society replete with people who don't believe they ever will be held accountable for their actions. If they did, the streets of the United States would be safer in 1997 than they were in 1776. But they aren't. If we are to change America's criminals, it is time the punishment publicly fit the crime. Let those who would beat their wives, steal their neighbor's property, and abuse children feel the sting of community intolerance, hear their names on our lips, and pay the price in view of the public. Shame on them or shame on us.

19. Whitney Wiedeman, *supra* note 16.

20. Mohamed Arafa & Jonathan Burns, *Judicial Corporal Punishment in the United States? Lessons From Islamic Criminal Law for Curing the Ills of Mass Incarceration*, 25 Ind. Int'l & Comp. L. Rev. 385 (2015).

21. *Id.*

22. Ole Martin Moen, *Judicial Corporal Punishment*, J. Ethics & Soc. Phil., 17, 27 (2020).

23. In Contemporary criminal justice system of Iran, flogging is available for variety of sexual offenses, crimes against the persons, crimes against the property, crimes against the public security and morals.

24. He was an American lawyer and jurist who served as an associate justice of the US Supreme Court from 1956 to 1990 and known for being a leader of the US Supreme Court's liberal wing.

25. Trop v. Dulles, 356 U.S. 86 (1958).

26. Graeme Newman, *supra* note 1, at 141.

Chapter 4

From Different Methods to International Restrictions

Many forms of corporal punishment are less burdensome than long-term incarceration.[1]

CORPORAL PUNISHMENT METHODS IN THE UNITED STATES AND IRAN

Whipping

Foremost among the bodily punishments was whipping. Whipping is also known as flogging, lashing, strapping, beating, or caning. All these methods involve striking the accused with an object to produce immediate and acute pain. Various tools have been used to flog people including metal rods, straps, branches, logs, whips, rubber hoses, cat-o-nine tails, and rattan canes.[2]

Whipping was a widely accepted form of punishment throughout the world at various times. In colonial America, it was meted out by the stripe. In other words, the accused were sentenced to twenty stripes, a stripe being the mark made by the whip on the accused. A limit of forty stripes at one time was recognized throughout the colonies. This limitation, like many other laws of the time, was biblical in origin and based on the Book of Deuteronomy: "Forty stripes he may give him, and not to exceed: lest, if he should exceed, and beat him above these many stripes, then thy brother should seem vile unto thee."

Regarding whipping, as well as the other bodily punishments, the higher the offender's socioeconomic status, the less likely the offender is to receive whipping punishments. In addition to the forty stripes limit, the Massachusetts Body of Liberties stated, ". . . nor shall neither any true gentleman, nor any man equal to a gentleman be punished with whipping, unless his crime be very shameful, and his course of life vicious and profligate."[3] Men of standing in the community would receive a fine, and even this would be remitted after a period of good behavior. Thus, whipping appears to have been reserved for those who could not afford to pay fines.

Whippings were administered in public as were all other forms of corporal punishment. The great majority of whippings took place at a centrally located whipping post where the offender was bound and the whip applied to his bare back.[4] If the crime was particularly offensive, the culprit was bound to the back of a cart and forced to walk behind it. The stripes were applied as the cart was pulled through the town.[5]

In colonial America, judges commonly sentenced criminals to the whipping post. Nearly every crime, no matter how petty, was punished by whipping. Whipping was abolished crime by crime, finally disappearing as late as 1986.[6]

In ancient Iran,[7] whipping was administered in the amount of 5 lashes to 250 lashes (200 lashes for poisoning a shepherd dog and 90 lashes for manslaughter). Judges could convert whipping punishment to a fine.[8] The following crimes had whipping as punishment: theft, violation of covenant, sodomy, unsuitable dog feeding, dog killing, heating the dog, carrying arms, causing wounds and injuries.[9] Whipping was practiced well before the Pahlavi Dynasty.[10] Following the reign of the Pahlavi monarchs, it was imposed for three crimes. Whipping was finally abolished in Iran in 1966. However, with Islamic government approval, whipping is permitted in Iran as indicated in figure 4.1.

The Islamic criminal justice system of Iran provides that a woman who appears in public without appropriate attire, such as a cloth scarf over the head (*hijab*) and a long jacket (*manteau*), or a large full-length cloth covering (*chador*), may be sentenced to flogging and fined. Absent a clear legal definition of "appropriate attire" or of the related punishment, women (and men)

Figure 4.1 Flogging in Islamic Penal Code of Iran. *Source*: Figure created by author.

were subjected to the opinions of various disciplinary and security force members, police, and judges.[11]

Authorities continued to arrest women for violating dress requirements, and courts applied harsh sentences.

> In February 2021 an appeals court upheld sentences of sixteen to twenty-three years for Yasaman Aryani, her mother Monireh Arabshahi, and Mojgan Keshavarz for "'spreading propaganda against the system'" and "inciting corruption and prostitution." They were arrested after posting a video for International Women's Day in 2019 during which they walked without headscarves through a Tehran metro train, handing flowers to female passengers. As of September 19, all three women remained in prison.

Branding

Serious offenses warranted branding. Branding was an alternative when it was necessary to mark the criminal so that those who might have later dealings with him would be put on notice. The practice of branding survived in England until at least 1699. The practice of branding was also adopted by the American colonies. In some colonies, branding was replaced with requiring offenders to conspicuously wear a badge or a sewn letter indicating the committed crime. Under the East Jersey Codes of 1668 and 1675, first convictions for burglary were punishable by the branding of a "T" on the hand, and second convictions for the same offense were punishable by the branding of an "R" on the forehead of the offender. The Maryland colony branded the letter "B" on the forehead of convicted blasphemers, and adulteresses were required to wear the "scarlet letter" in many New England colonies. The letter "A" sewn to the adulterer's clothing was common, but some victims were branded with the letter.[12] Branding, ear cropping, piercing, and burning of tongues, and similar forms of punishment continued until at least the time of the American Revolution.[13]

Mutilation

Mutilation was another example of early punishment used in England and later administered in the American colonies. There were three classes of punitive mutilation. First, where punishment mirrored the crime committed, the *lex talionis* method of punishment was administered. Mayhem was met with mayhem—an eye for an eye. The second class included cases where the government removed the offending appendage. For example, thieves had their hands severed, and perjurers had their tongues removed. This type of punishment dates to at least 1700 BC.[14] Finally, in early European history, severe and brutal mutilations were used solely for retribution and deterrence purposes. In such cases, there was no proportionality between crime and mutilation. Noses, ears, and lips were slit; eyes were plucked out; and scalps were torn from the heads of offenders. Mutilating punishment reserved for serious offenses was the cutting off one or both ears. The cropping of ears was not always neatly accomplished. Sometimes the ears were nailed to the pillory (a description of this device to follow) during the prisoner's stay there. When the prisoner's time was up, he was permitted to leave; his ears, however, were expected to stay.[15]

Other mutilating punishments, popular in England and on the European continent at the time, such as slitting nostrils, removing noses and scalps, and cutting out or piercing tongues with hot irons, never received widespread acceptance in the colonies.[16] This is not to say that tongues were totally safe. Lying, mild blasphemy, and gossip were punishable by fastening a cleft stick to the tongue to prevent talking. The offender was then made to stand in some public place in that condition so that all could see his predicament. An alternative to the cleft stick was gagging. Again, the gagged individual was made to stand in public in that condition.[17]

Mutilation was not a common punishment in ancient Persia. It was practiced for crimes involving usurper theft, abortion, and adultery. Blinding was a punishment for rebellious princes achieved by dipping hot needles in the eyes of criminals. These punishments were imposed only by the king's sentence.[18] Under Islamic laws, mutilation was punishment for a special kind of theft (*hadd* Theft),[19] resorting to arms to frighten people (*moharebeh),*[20] and organ retaliation (*qisas*) for injuries.[21]

For example, in October 2021, a court in Tehran sentenced a man to be blinded in one eye under the principle of "retribution-in-kind" (*qisas*) for assault. Mutilation punishments are rare in practice. (Please see chart 4.2).

Ducking Stool

The ducking stool was not at all a popular means of punishment. The ducking stool was a device in which the prisoner was restrained and repeatedly dunked in water. The device itself was complicated to build and had to be built near a body of water sufficiently deep enough to submerge the victim.

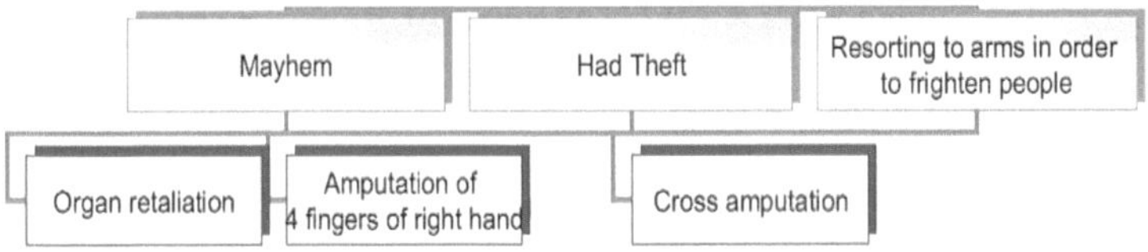

For this ***Theft*** 16 special conditions must be proven: puberty and sanity for thief, without threat and coercion on thief, intention for theft, knowledge that property belongs to somebody else, knowledge that this act is unlawful, property should be located in the safe custody, breaking to the safe custody, the minimum value of property, lack of necessity for the theft, thief is not the father of the owner, safe custody had not belonged to thief previously, the act is for stealing, lack of famine, proportionate of safe custody, and stolen goods are not government property unknown ownership.

Figure 4.2 Mutilation in Islamic Penal Code of Iran. *Source*: Figure created by author.

The necessity for a deep body of water conflicted with the desire that the punishment be in a central public place so that the greatest percentage of the community could view the spectacle. Thus, while there is evidence of the existence of the ducking stool in colonial America, there is little evidence of its actual use.[22] Most often women received the ducking stool as a punishment. Gossips, slanderers, public scolds, and unruly women were ducked. Although the ducking stool was used primarily to punish women, men were also subject to the punishment. Men who had committed the offense of public drunkenness, had sold bad bread or beer, had caused disturbances, or had brutally beaten their wives were dunked. Georgia sentenced people to the ducking stool as late as 1811.[23]

Stocks and the Pillory

The stocks and the pillory were used when it was felt that public shame and humiliation would best serve justice.[24] By the seventeenth century, though, the humiliating effect of sitting in the stocks was being utilized as a punishment. The stock held prisoners in a seated position with their legs and hands secured. The pillory held the prisoner in a standing position with head and hands secured in a locked frame. Offenders were subject to public ridicule, pelting, and stoning while held in either the stock or the pillory. In some cases, the prisoner received an additional form of punishment, such as flogging or branding, while he was confined to the stock or the pillory. For example, in the case of the pillory, as described above, the ears of the offender were nailed to the pillory, and, when the time for release came, the offender would either tear his ears loose or the ears would be severed by the official in charge. Both the stock and pillory were commonly used during colonial times and the times following the ratification of the Constitution. The use of the pillory survived until as late as 1905.[25]

INTERNATIONAL ASPECT

Treaties and International Cases

Multiple existing international human rights documents prohibit torture and cruel, inhuman, or degrading punishment:

The oldest of the existing conventions is the Universal Declaration of Human Rights, adopted in 1948, which protects individuals from torture and cruel, inhuman, or degrading punishment. Since the Universal Declaration, the United Nations ratified the Convention for the Protection of Human Rights and Fundamental Freedoms in 1950, followed by the International Convention on Civil and Political Rights in 1966. Both conventions also contain provisions prohibiting cruel or torturous punishment. While the three aforementioned documents are general conventions addressing various human rights issues, a more recent agreement specifically centers on addressing concerns related to punishment.[26] Article 5 of the Universal Declaration of Human Rights provides that "no one shall be subjected to torture or to cruel, inhuman or degrading treatment or punishment."

Article 7 of the International Covenant on Civil and Political Rights (ICCPR) provides that "no one shall be subjected to torture or to cruel, inhuman or degrading treatment or punishment. In particular, no one shall be subjected without his free consent to medical or scientific experimentation." Article 10, paragraph 1 of the ICCPR states that "all persons deprived of their liberty shall be treated with humanity and with respect for the inherent dignity of the human person." The United Nations Human Rights Committee, in its authoritative general comment on Article 7 of the ICCPR, emphasized that the absolute prohibition of cruel, inhuman, or degrading punishment must extend to corporal punishment.

Article 5 of the American Convention on Human Rights[27] provides:

1. every person has the right to have his physical, mental, and moral integrity respected.
2. No one shall be subjected to torture or to cruel, inhuman, or degrading punishment or treatment. All persons deprived of their liberty shall be treated with respect for the inherent dignity of the human person.

Also, Article 5 of the African Charter of Human Rights[28] provides:

Every individual shall have the right to the respect of the dignity inherent in a human being and to the recognition of his legal status. All forms of exploitation and degradation of man, particularly slavery, slave trade, torture, cruel, inhuman, or degrading punishment and treatment shall be prohibited.

Various international cases have dealt with corporal punishment. Courts have, however, ruled that whipping and flogging violate international law, but only as punishments for property crimes. Although the European Court of Human Rights held that "birching" in the Isle of Man violated international human rights, the European Commission of Human Rights concluded that corporal punishment in Scottish schools did not.[29]

In *Campbell & Cosans v. United Kingdom*,[30] two plaintiffs filed separate applications with the European Commission, each contending that the use of corporal punishment violated Article 3.[31] The court recognized that a mere threat of prohibited conduct may violate Article 3. Nevertheless, the court found that the mere threat of corporal punishment did not meet the minimum level of severity as defined in *Ireland v. United Kingdom*. In the present case, no punishment has been inflicted. "Treatment itself will not be degrading unless the person concerned has undergone—either in the eyes of others or in his own eyes—humiliation or debasement attaining a minimum level of severity."[32]

To determine whether the boys experienced humiliation or debasement, the court noted that a threat directed to an exceptionally insensitive person may have no significant effect on him but nevertheless be incontrovertibly degrading; and conversely, an exceptionally sensitive person might be deeply affected by a threat that could be described as degrading only by a distortion of the ordinary and usual meaning of the word.[33]

The preceding cases illustrate that conduct must transcend a minimum level of severity to merit judicial review. To determine whether particular conduct meets that standard, the court examines the totality of circumstances. It considers the "nature and context of the punishment itself and the manner and method of its execution,"[34] as well as the prospective physical and psychological effects on the individual.[35]

Amnesty International

Amnesty International repeats the proclamation that caning is torture. Amnesty International take a stance against the use of corporal punishment as a violation of the right not to be subjected to torture or cruel, inhuman, or degrading treatment or punishment guaranteed by Article 5 of the Universal Declaration of Human Rights.

Amnesty International understands that there is a need for effective deterrents against rape and that rape is a truly repugnant crime, the perpetrators of which should be brought to justice. However, the organization believes that no crime, no matter how serious, justifies the use of punishments that constitute torture or cruel, degrading, or inhuman treatment.[36]

Amnesty International considers that the imposition of corporal punishment is also contrary to Articles 7 and 10(1) of the ICCPR: Article 7: "No one shall be subjected to torture or to cruel, inhuman or degrading treatment or punishment. In particular, no one shall be subjected without his free consent to medical or scientific experimentation." Article 10: "All persons deprived of their liberty shall be treated with humanity and with respect for the inherent dignity of the human person." In its General Comment 20 on Article 7, the Committee emphasized that the absolute prohibition of cruel, inhuman, or degrading punishment in Article 7 of the ICCPR "must extend to corporal punishment." This contention is strongly supported by other expert bodies and international jurisprudence.[37]

Applying International Norms in Domestic Courts

There are three principal means by which domestic courts have applied or incorporated international law as a part of their domestic legal system: (1) by directly applying the terms of international treaties entered into by their respective governments; (2) by using international law to guide the interpretation of the state's own domestic law; and (3) by applying customary international law.[38] In countries which have incorporated international human rights law into their own jurisprudence, an appeal can be made directly to international law in a domestic case. Countries differ substantially in the extent to which they incorporate international law directly into their national law. Some countries such as Austria, Belgium, the Netherlands, and Romania accept international law as equal to, or supreme over, their own domestic law. Other countries, such as the United Kingdom, do not consider international law to be judicially enforceable unless it is implemented by domestic legislation.

The United States combines these two approaches.[39] There is significant interplay among these different ways of applying international law domestically, and it is somewhat artificial to discuss these forms of incorporating international law under discrete rubrics. For example, the acceptance of a treaty by a wide number of nations may lead a court to accept a treaty provision as part of customary international law and apply such provisions domestically even if the nation has not signed the treaty.[40]

> One of the contemporary examples is the caning of an American teenager Michael Fay in Singapore has prompted worldwide debate over the international laws governing criminal punishment. Michael Fay was sentenced to six strokes of the cane in Singapore in 1994 for theft of road signs and vandalizing eighteen cars over a ten-day period in September 1993.

Although international law consistently prohibits torture and cruel, inhuman, or degrading punishment, the question remains whether caning fits in that category of punishment. Although American medical organizations, including the American Medical Association (AMA), condemn the presence of doctors at canings, their presence is one element of Singapore's caning laws which distinguishes caning from cruel and inhuman punishment. By restricting the class of people eligible for caning, requiring the presence of doctors at canings, and establishing the size and type of instrument that constitutes a cane, Singapore's laws safeguard citizens from cruel, inhuman, or degrading punishment. Although the West condemns Singapore's punishment of caning as cruel and inhuman, the West must remember that the Republic of Singapore is only around sixty years old. In addition, caning does not always violate international prohibitions against torture and cruel, inhuman, or degrading punishment. Although international law prohibits torture and cruel, inhuman, or degrading punishment, caning is no crueler and more inhuman than capital punishment which is regularly practiced by the United States.[41]

Applying international standards to US legal principles may be problematic. In *Stanford v. Kentucky,*[42] Judge William Rehnquist, writing his plurality opinion, stated neither norms nor the legal standards of other countries should disposition the Eighth Amendment. The government believes domestic laws provide more protection than international treaties and customary laws. Furthermore, even if the United States were to adopt the international definition of torture, application of this norm to lawful sanctions may be inappropriate. The Convention on Torture, for example, states, "[torture] does not involve pain or suffering arising only from, inherent in or incidental to lawful sanctions." For example, since capital punishment is legal in the United States, this treaty would not forbid states from using methods of execution which involve torturous treatment. As a result, the treaty becomes a futile attempt to satisfy human rights activists.[43]

However, while it is reasonable for judges to grant national standards greater influence when assessing what is cruel and unusual, judges should allow international trends to shed light on the issue as well. Especially because the United States is a party to international agreements that bear on the issue, it seems legally necessary to consider international trends at least relevant to an inquiry into contemporary standards of decency.

The United States is, of course, a founding participant in and the permanent host of the United Nations, the preamble of whose charter lists among the purposes of the organization, to reaffirm faith in fundamental human rights, [and] in the dignity and worth of the human person, and to promote social progress and better standards of life. Furthermore, in 1994, the United States ratified the Convention against Torture and Other Cruel, Inhuman, or Degrading Treatment or Punishment. However, in ratifying the latter Convention and other such international instruments calling for adherence to international human rights standards, the United States has attached reservations intended to keep these pacts from forcing any change in United States law or policy.

However, reservations are designed to reject any obligation to rise above existing law and practice of dubious propriety. Even friends of the United States have objected that its reservations are incompatible with that object and purpose and are therefore invalid.

Setting aside the valid question of whether American law is subject to international human rights standards by force of these instruments of international law, the assent of the United States generally to the UN Charter and to various treaties and international agreements promoting the dignity and worth of the human person and social progress suggests strongly that the United States has opened the door to the influence of the international community in assessing contemporary standards of decency.[44]

In contrast to the international community, the United States adheres to a cruel and unusual punishment clause. The Supreme Court interprets this clause by determining the "evolving standards of decency." International norms are indicative of the view of the global community on specific issues. As already mentioned, the international community has spoken on the issue of torture and called for a ban on such practices. Application of a world opinion gives a greater indication of the "evolving standards of decency" than does the regional bias of separate jury panels and state criminal codes. Therefore, using international norms will not invade our sovereignty but will provide a better guideline in deciding what cruel and unusual punishment is.[45]

In Iran, Islamic penal law sets forth several crimes and penalties that are the object of criticism from the international human rights community. These penalties, although protecting Islamic religious principles, mete out harsh penalties that violate the right to life and, in many cases, may reach the threshold of torture or cruel, inhuman, or degrading punishment.

International human rights discourse texts do not discuss punishments for specific violations of criminal law. However, the prohibition against torture would apply to death by crucifixion and cross amputation. A death sentence might be acceptable if able to be carried out in a humane manner for particularly serious acts. Forcibly expelling a convicted brigand from his country with no right to ever return may violate international norms.

Judicial corporal punishment in the forms of flogging and amputation for the offenses of theft, alcohol consumption, robbery, adultery, and rape in Islamic criminal justice systems constitute torture or cruel, inhuman, or degrading punishment under Article 7 of the ICCPR (for more information please refer to chapter 6).

Despite international human rights treaties to which Iran is a party, there are several cases documented by Amnesty International where courts have ordered amputations for theft and robbery. Iranian courts have ordered public floggings. These severe penalties have forced dissenters subject to *Sharia* law to renounce Islam, reflecting the internal dissent among Muslims that has resulted from the adoption of *Sharia* penal law in Iran.

> In July 2017, Amnesty International reported the public flogging of a man in Niazmand Square, Kashmar, Razavi Khorasan Province, for a sentence he had received ten years before for consuming alcohol at a wedding when he was fourteen to fifteen years old. National media outlets posted a picture showing the man roped to a tree, lashed by a masked man and his back covered in blood, with a crowd of persons watching.

The crime of robbery is considered one of the most serious crimes under *Sharia* law. *Moharebeh* is punishable by amputation of the right hand for the first offense, amputation of the left foot for a second offense, life imprisonment for a third offense, and death penalty for a fourth offense.[46] These penalties are seriously contested by members of the international human rights community, such as Human Rights Watch, as violations of the right to life and the right to be free from torture or cruel, unusual, or degrading punishment. Furthermore, these crimes are not uniquely offensive to an Islamic value system but constitute common crimes that require regulation by a standard system of law enforcement.

Flogging may cause severe pain or suffering, but it is a lawful sanction in Iran. Similarly, the death penalty causes severe pain and suffering and is considered cruel and unusual by the European Court on Human Rights.[47] The death penalty remains in practice as a legal sanction in the United States and Iran. Consequently, a comparison between flogging in Iran and the death penalty in the United States reveals that both countries are potentially guilty of violating international law.

The UN Special Reporter on Torture states corporal punishment is inconsistent with the prohibition of torture and other cruel, inhuman, or degrading treatment or punishment.[48] The UN Human Rights Committee found that corporal punishment is excessive under Article 7 of the ICCPR, which prohibits cruel, inhuman, or degrading treatment.[49] According to the language in the international human rights treaties to which Iran is bound, corporal punishment provided for in the Islamic Penal Code does not adequately protect the rights of Iranian citizens to be free from cruel, inhuman, or degrading treatment.

According to General Comment 22, freedom of religion[50] is wholly protected to the extent that it does not infringe on other fundamental rights protected by the ICCPR. In terms of consistency, the Islamic criminal justice system conflicts with Iran's international human rights obligations. A state is not prohibited from adopting an official religion, but it must not infringe on the rights of others to practice their own religions or profess no faith at all. This provision in the ICCPR is particularly relevant because non-Muslims and some Muslims prefer to be judged under secular criminal justice system rather than an Islamic criminal justice system.

Iran is party to several international human rights treaties, which bind Iran to respect and ensure the human rights of all individuals within its territory. Iran is a party to the ICCPR. In addition, a number of international instruments such as the Universal Declaration of Human Rights and the Declaration on the Rights of Persons Belonging to National or Ethnic, Religious, and Linguistic Minorities (Minorities Declaration) are binding as customary international law.

According to Article 14 of the Vienna Convention on the Law of Treaties,[51] once international treaties have been ratified a state party is bound to carry out its international obligations and may not invoke its domestic law as justification for non-implementation. Thus, the government of Iran has the ultimate responsibility to ensure that human rights are respected in the territory of Iran. As a result, the Islamic Penal Code is not a valid reason for non-implementation of Iran's international human rights obligations.

Indeed, the prohibition of torture is a peremptory norm of international law which means it applies to all countries, whether they have consented to be bound by it. As such, it can protect the citizens of a country that has not signed any of the international instruments prohibiting cruel punishment.

Thus, the utilization of the definition of the international norm of torture is more indicative of the "evolving standards of decency" rather than the opinions of juries and legislatures. The international norm displays the opinion of the global community giving the national courts a better interpretation than the regional decision making of juries and state governments.[52]

NOTES

1. Ole Martin Moen, *Judicial Corporal Punishment*, 17 J. Ethics & Soc. Phil., 27 (2020).
2. Robert G. Caldwell, *Criminology*, 451–452 (2d ed. 1965).
3. Edwin Powers, *Crime and Punishment in Early Massachusetts: 1620-1692*, 254 (Boston: Beacon Press, 1966).
4. Alice Earle Morse, *Curious Punishments of Bygone Days*, 70–85 (Chicago: Herbert S. Stone and Company, 1896).
5. Edwin Powers, *supra* note 3, at 174.
6. *Id.*
7. Ancient Iran, historically known as Persia, was the dominant nation of western Asia foe over a millennium (about 550 BC-AD 650).
8. Mohammad Bagher Karami, *Introduction on Criminal Justice System in Ancient Iran*, 57 (Khate sevvom, 1380).

9. Parviz Saneiee, *General Criminal Law,* 287 (Iran, Tehran: Ganje Danesh Publication, Fall 1992).

10. The Pahlavi dynasty was the last Iranian royal dynasty, ruling for almost fifty-four years between 1925 and 1979.

11. US Department of State, Country Reports on Human Rights (2021).

12. Daniel Hall, *When Canning Meets the Eighth Amendment: Whipping Offenders in the United States*, 4 Widenr J. Pub. L. 403 (1995).

13. See Mitchel P. Roth, *Crime and Punishment: A History of the Criminal Justice System*, p 54-55, Thomson Wadsworth, CA (2005).

14. Drapkin Israel, *Crime and Punishment in the Ancient World*, 26 (Lexington Bks, 1989).

15. *Id.*

16. Steven A. Hatfield, *Criminal Punishment in America: From the Colonial to the Modern Era, 1* USAFA J. Leg. Stud. 181 (1990).

17. Edwin Powers, *supra* note 3, at 185.

18. Ava Vahedi, *Criminal Justice System in Sasanian Era*, 86–87 (Mizan publication, 1380) [in Farsi].

19. Islamic Penal Code of Iran, Art 201 (1991) [In Farsi].

20. *Id,* Art 183.

21. *Id,* Art 269.

22. Edwin Powers, *supra* note 3.

23. Daniel Hall, *supra note* 12.

24. Graeme Newman, *Just and Painful: A Case for the Corporal Punishment of Criminals*, 114 (Macmillan Publishing Company, 1983).

25. Daniel Hall, *supra* note 12.

26. See Convention Against Torture and Other Cruel, Inhuman or Degrading Treatment or Punishment, 39 U.N. GAOR, 39th Sess., Supp. No. 51, at 197, U.N. Doc. A/RES/39/46 (1984); Universal Declaration of Human Rights, G.A. Res. 217 (III), U.N. GAOR, 3d Sess., at 71, U.N. Doc. A/810 (1948) Freedoms, Nov. 4, 1950, 213 U.N.T.S. 221]; International Covenant on Civil and Political Rights, G.A. Res. 2200 (XXI), U.N. GAOR, 21st Sess., Supp. No. 16, at 52, U.N. Doc. A/6316 (1966).

27. Nov. 22, 1969, O.A.S. Treaty Series No. 36, O.A.S. Official Records OEA/Ser. L/V/II, Doc. 21, rev. 6 (1970).

28. African [Banjul] Charter on Human and Peoples' Rights, adopted June 27, 1981, OAU Doc. CAB/LEG/67/3 rev. 5, 21 I.L.M. 58 (1982), *entered into force* Oct. 21 (1986).

29. Jordan J. Paust, *Human Dignity as a Constitutional Right: A Jurisprudentially Based Inquiry into Criteria and Content*, 27 How. L.J. 145, 176 (1984).

30. Campbell & Cosans v. United Kingdom, 48 Eur. Ct. H.R. (ser. A) (1982).

31. Campbell attended a school that disciplined students using corporal punishment. The Regional Education Council refused to guarantee that Campbell would not face such measures. Cosans also attended a school that used corporal punishment. He was to receive punishment for allegedly taking a prohibited shortcut through a cemetery on his way home from school.

32. Ireland v. United Kingdom, 25 Eur. Ct. H.R. (ser. A) at 66 (1978) ("The [European] Convention, with its distinction between 'torture' and 'inhuman or degrading treatment', should by the first of these terms attach a special stigma to deliberate inhuman treatment causing very serious and cruel suffering.").

33. *Id.*

34. Campbell & Cosans, 48 Eur. Ct. H.R.

35. Tyrer v. United Kingdom, 26 Eur. Ct. H.R. (ser. A) At 15, 17 (1978).

36. See www.amnesty.org.

37. For example, the UN Commission on Human Rights, resolution 1997/38 of April 1997; Nigel Rodley, Special Rapporteur on Torture, in his report to the Commission on Human Rights, January 10, 1997, E/CN.4/1997/7; the European Court of Human Rights in Tyrer v. The United Kingdom, Application no. 2865/72, European Court of Human Rights, Series B, No. 24.

38. Article 38(1) of the Statute of the International Court of Justice identifies the sources of international law: (a) treaties, (b) international custom, as evidence of a general practice accepted as law (customary international law), (c) general principles of law, and (d) judicial decisions and teachings of the most highly qualified publicists. 1947 I.C.J. Acts & Docs. 77. See also Restatement (Third) of the Foreign Relations Law of the United States, s102 (1) (1987).

39. In the United States, a treaty ratified by the United States is part of the supreme law of the land, of equal dignity with federal statutes. Article VI, paragraph 2 of the US Constitution states the following: This Constitution, and the Laws of the United States which shall be made in Pursuance thereof; and all Treaties made, or which shall be made under the Authority of the United States, shall be the supreme Law of the Land; and the Judges in every State shall be bound thereby, any Thing in the Constitution or Laws of any State to the Contrary notwithstanding. (Emphasis added). Conflicts between treaty clauses and existing U.S. law are resolved according to three rules, (1) a treaty may not infringe on certain provisions of the U.S. Constitution, Reid v. Covert, 354 U.S. 1 (1957); (2) if there is a conflict between a treaty and a federal statute, the more recent prevails, and (3) if there is a conflict between a treaty and state law, the treaty controls, Zschernig v. Miller, 389 U.S. 429, 440–441 (1968). Customary law enjoys, in theory, a status under United States law similar to the US Constitution, although there is some controversy over whether it is in fact equal in status. US courts have, nevertheless, recognized the domestic authority of international customary law in certain cases. See The Paquete Habana, 175 U.S. 677, 700 (1900) (customary law is "part of our law, and must be ascertained and administered by the courts of justice of appropriate jurisdiction as often as questions of right depending upon it are duly presented for their determination"). In one of the most important cases to address the issue of domestic application of customary international law, the court in Filartiga v. Pena-Irala, 630 F.2d 876 (2d Cir. 1980), stated that "where the nations of the world have adopted a norm in terms so formal and unambiguous as to make it international 'law,' the interests of the global community transcend those of any one state." The Circuit Court noted that "although there is no universal agreement as to the precise extent of the 'human rights and fundamental freedoms' guaranteed to all by the U.N. Charter, there is at present no dissent from the view that guaranties

include, at a bare minimum, the right to be free from torture. This prohibition has become part of customary international law, as evidenced and defined by the Universal Declaration of Human Rights." (Emphasis added). In Committee of United States' Citizens Living in Nicaragua v. Reagan, 859 F.2d 929 (D.C. Cir. 1988), the Circuit Court noted the supremacy of peremptory norms of international law (jus cogens) over domestic and customary international law. The court stated in dicta that "[s]uch basic norms of international law as the proscription against murder and slavery may well . . . restrain our government in the same way that the Constitution restrains it. If Congress adopted a foreign policy that resulted in the enslavement of our citizens or other individuals that policy might well be subject to challenge in domestic court under international law."

40. For example, with respect to the Vienna Convention on the Law of Treaties, the legal advisor of the US Department of State wrote a Letter of Submittal to the president in which he stated: While the United States has not yet ratified the Vienna Convention on the Law of Treaties, [the United States has] consistently appl[ied] those of its terms which constitute a codification of customary international law. Most provisions of the Vienna Convention, including Articles 31 and 32 on matters of treaty interpretation, are declaratory of customary international law. Marian L. Nash, *Contemporary Practice of the United States Relating to International Law*, 75 Am. J. Int'l L. 142, 147, reprinted in Newman & Weissbrodt (1981).

41. Firouzeh Bahrampour, *Note and Comment: The Canning of Michael Fay: Can Singapore's Punishment withstand the Scrutiny of International Law*, 10 Am. U.J. Int'l L. & Pol'y 1057 (1995).

42. Stanford v. Kentucky, 109 S. Ct. 2969, 2975 (1989).

43. Garry Ledbetter, *The International Norms: An Interpretation of the "Evolving Standard of Decency,"* 2 San Diego Justice J. 263 (1994).

44. Steven Manley, *The Constitution. The Punishment of death, and Misguided Originalism,* 1999 L. Rev. M.S.U. D.C.L. 913 (1999).

45. *Id.*

46. Islamic Penal Code of Iran, Art 201 (1991) [In Farsi].

47. See M. Cherif Bassiouni, *Human Rights in the Context of Criminal Justice: Identifying International Procedural Protections and Equivalent Protections in National Constitutions, 3 Duke J. Comp. & Int'l L.* 235, 262–263, nn.118–128 (1993) (observing that the right to freedom from torture and cruel, inhuman, or degrading punishment appears in numerous international agreements as well as eighty-one national constitutions). Also, see Highet and Kahale, (citingTyrer v. United Kingdom, 26 Eur. Ct. H.R. (1978) (ruling that the punishment of birching is degrading and therefore violates the European Convention on Human Rights); Warwick v. United Kingdom, Eur. Comm'n H.R., Report of July 18, 1986 (unreported) (holding that corporal punishment, even one cane stroke on the hand, is degrading and violates the European Convention on Human Rights).

48. See http://www.universalhumanrightsindex.org/documents/843/802/document/fr/text.html.

49. *Id.*

50. General Comment No. 22: The right to freedom of thought, conscience and religion (Art. 18) 30/07/93. CCPR/C/21/Rev.1/Add.4, General Comment No. 22.

51. Vienna Convention on the Law of Treaties, May 23, 1969, 1155 U.N.T.S. 331; 8 I.L.M. 679 (1969).

52. Garry Ledbetter, *supra* note 43.

Chapter 5

Contemporary Use of Corporal Punishments

وَالسَّارِقُ وَالسَّارِقَةُ فَاقْطَعُوا أَيْدِيَهُمَا جَزَاءً بِمَا كَسَبَا نَكَالًا مِّنَ اللَّهِ ۗ وَاللَّهُ عَزِيزٌ حَكِيمٌ

> As for a man or woman who commits theft, cut off the hands of both to recompense them for what they earned, a deterrent from Allah. And Allah is Mighty, Wise.[1]

OVERVIEW

At the beginning of the twenty-first century, corporal punishment is no longer a legal sanction in most countries around the world. Judicial corporal punishment is almost nonexistent today in industrialized democratic countries, except for disciplining children in families and schools. At the same time, in some countries judicial corporal punishment has been retained and even extended.

At least twenty-seven nations punish offenders with judicial corporal punishment. *Newsweek* reported that the laws of the following nations provide for judicial corporal punishment: Afghanistan, Antigua and Barbuda, Bahamas, Barbados, Botswana, Brunei, Dominica, Indonesia, Iran, Libya, Malaysia, Maldives, Mauritania, Nigeria (Provinces with Islamic criminal justice system), Pakistan, Qatar, Saudi Arabia, Singapore, Somalia, St. Kitts and Nevis, St. Vincent and the Grenadines, Tanzania, Trinidad and Tobago, Tonga, Tuvalu, United Arab Emirates, and Yemen. Of the twenty-seven countries, twelve of them have Islamic criminal justice systems and fourteen of them are Islamic nations. Other countries, especially former colonies of England, use judicial corporal punishments to punish juvenile offenders, and Latin American countries have this punishment as a traditional form of justice. From retentionist countries, seven of them are located in the Americas, six in East Asia and Pacific, six in the Middle East and North Africa, four in Africa, and three in South Asia.[2]

The recent trend in the United States reflects a desire to impose stricter punishments like those of Iran and other retentionists nations.[3] It has already been shown that early American courts approved of whipping. The same is true of the contemporary courts that have considered the issue, with one major exception. Courts have reviewed the use of corporal punishment by prison authorities to discipline inmates by whipping them and have concluded that corporal punishment is not unconstitutional per se.

In the wake of rising crime rates, an increase in the number of youthful offenders, a growing public dissatisfaction with the prison system and the rehabilitative corrections model, and media accounts of the success of foreign systems using a retributive approach in deterring crime, the possible use of corporal punishment in the United States has evoked the public's interest. In addition to the popular interest, several public officials have considered the use of corporal punishment, especially for youthful offenders.[4] John Gleissner, who is a writer and an attorney in Alabama, states

> The effectiveness and efficiency of JCP[5] in deterring crime, allowing rehabilitation, and achieving visible retribution will eventually decide its fate in the U.S. as an additional punishment option. Only the passage of JCP legislation for a period of time sufficient to establish its benefits and disadvantages in our society fairly tests this mode of punishment in light of scientific advancements and social developments during its disuse.[6]

Two states may have provided the avenue toward reinstituting whipping as a viable form of punishment. Maryland and Mississippi introduced bills that would provide for whipping if enacted into law,[7] and several other states have considered it in the past. In Maryland, juveniles aged fourteen and older could be caned up to ten times with a rattan cane for stealing or destroying property worth more than $300 and for other serious crimes. The legislation proposed in Mississippi would amend the state constitution and grant the legislature the authority to use caning to punish the convict for appropriate criminal convictions.[8] In addition, whipping has been considered in at least four other jurisdictions.

Since California first proposed its paddling bill, at least eight other states attempted to pass similar legislation. Various versions of paddling laws were introduced in Missouri, New Mexico, and New York. Some states, including Louisiana, Mississippi, and Tennessee, have even considered public canings for a series of property crimes including vandalism. The most radical proposal, however, was the Arkansas bill that would allow jury-sanctioned public hangings.[9] This recent renewed interest can be at least partially credited to the 1994 caning of Michael Fay in Singapore for vandalism.[10] His case has made people willing to reexamine why corporal punishment fell into such disfavor.

Surprisingly, a poll conducted after the canning of Michael Fay in Singapore indicates a large swath of US opinion delighted in vandal Fay getting swatted multiple times by Singaporean officials. This poll was conducted by *Los Angeles Times* in 1994, 49% of American said they approve of the sentence, which President Clinton has protested, while 48% disapprove of Singapore carrying it out. But poll respondents were much less willing to imagine using such punishment in America. Just 36% said they would approve of caning "for teenage vandals here in the United States." Three in five said they would disapprove. On the question of whether Singapore should carry out the sentence, sharp racial and gender differences emerged. Men approved the decision to cane Fay 61% to 36%, while women disapproved 58% to 39%. Whites narrowly favored the sentence by 52% to 45%, while 55% of blacks and 58% of Latinos opposed it. By contrast, a majority of men and women, whites, blacks, and Latinos all opposed using the punishment here, although the level of opposition was greater among women and Latinos.[11]

Some scholars suggest that we can adopt *Halachic* corporal punishment. *Halachic* corporal punishment, or flogging, was the standard form of punishment for crimes that did not have biblically prescribed penalties. There were two forms of flogging, biblical and rabbinic. Biblical flogging was limited to thirty-nine lashes and served as a metaphoric substitute for the death penalty. Rabbinic whipping served to discipline an offender who had flouted a rabbinic precept and was not limited to a specific number of lashes. Theoretically, a candidate for rabbinic whipping could be flogged to death.[12]

The Talmudic scholars applied three unique procedures to corporal punishment. First, all whipping candidates received a physical examination immediately before being flogged. Only those deemed physically able to withstand the beating were lashed. Second, *Halachic* corporal punishment was imposed publicly to promote deterrence. Third, the sentencing judges had to attend and monitor the imposition of corporal punishment. Their presence ensured that the whipper did not whip excessively and if criminals became ill during punishment, whipping would cease. These requirements established that *Halachic* corporal punishment was not a form of torture or cruel and unusual punishment but served as both general and specific deterrent. It may be because *Halachic* corporal punishment was both a humane act and an effective deterrent. However, exactly copying *Halachic* punishment methods by the American legislature and judiciary would be inappropriate because American legal society can benefit from Talmudic penology by adapting sanctions modeled after the principles of *Halachic* punishment.[13]

USE OF CORPORAL PUNISHMENTS IN ISLAMIC CRIMINAL JUSTICE SYSTEMS

What Is Islamic Criminal Justice System?

The judicial corporal punishments such as flogging and mutilation of the body in Islamic countries are familiar to most readers because corporal punishment exists in the domestic law of most Islamic nations, but the ways by which these states employ corporal punishments are varied and inconsistent. With the Islamization of laws in the 1970s, more and more Islamic states began objecting to international norms for human rights and the abolition of harsh Islamic punishments, as being contrary to *Sharia*, the historically formulated traditional law of Islam.

The question is why contemporary Islamic penal systems are so cruel and short on mercy when in secular criminal justice systems efforts are made to guarantee that prisoners are treated humanely. This comparative study reaches back to classical Islam and the contemporary use of *Sharia* law in Islamic countries to trace how and why punishments in Islamic nations came to diverge.

Today, the majority of countries in the world have now abolished the judicial corporal punishments in law or practice. Of the twenty-seven retentionist countries, fourteen of them are Islamic countries.

Geographically six of these Islamic countries are in the Middle East. It is estimated that there are over 900 million Muslims today. Many live in the Arab world, but many more live in countries such as Iran, Pakistan, Bangladesh, Indonesia, Malaysia, Nigeria, and Sudan.[14] Although all Islamic countries are not retentionist, the practice varies considerably from one to another. For instance, some Islamic countries, like Iran and Saudi Arabia, are enthusiastic practitioners, with many cases of flogging and mutilation of body, while others, such as Qatar and United Arab Emirates, conduct these harsh punishments in only the rarest of cases; Islamic countries such as Albania, Azerbaijan, and Turkey have abolished corporal punishments. The diversity of practice would suggest there is little consensus among Islamic countries.

Countries that practice *Sharia* law as the source of their criminal justice system are associated with the use of judicial corporal punishments as retribution for the largest variety of crimes. Therefore, among Islamic nations we should distinguish Islamic states with Islamic criminal justice systems in which *Sharia* law or Islamic law is a form of legislation (e.g., Iran) with a state religion, in which Islam as the official religion of a country, where Islamic courts may be used (e.g., Malaysia), and secular criminal justice systems in which government institutions are separated from the role of religion (e.g., Turkey).

Although based on Islamic law, judicial corporal punishment is a mandatory penalty under the *Sharia* for a variety of crimes, and under penal codes of Islamic criminal justice systems flogging and mutilation of body have been prescribed for several crimes, practice of these punishments in Islamic countries is rare.

Degradation in judicial corporal punishments is related to some complex patterns in history and social development. If we want to maintain why some Islamic countries have abolished these harsh punishments, we need to examine how different social traditions have emerged. A major difficulty is how to distinguish cruel and unusual punishments in religious and secular criminal justice systems. The most dramatic differences are related to the proportionality doctrine. Penal proportionality based on religious proportionality in Islam is completely different from the secular proportionality in the Western countries. For example, the punishment of fornication in *Sharia* which is 100 lashes as stated in the Holy Quran would not pass the secular proportionality doctrine. In the secular countries, criminalizing conduct is related to harm, not to the virtue of Muslims.

When discussing punishments in Islamic criminal justice systems, keep in mind the relationship between the state and the concept of justice is derived from the religious principle of Islam. The *Sharia*, the general and particular rules of Islamic *corpus juris*, is not just a code of law but a code of conduct of behavior and ethics, a combination of law and morality, inseparable. Evidence of this relationship can be seen in the penal code and punishments of the following Islamic countries: Mauritania, Somalia, Sudan, Afghanistan, Brunei, Iran, Iraq, Maldives, Pakistan, Qatar, Saudi Arabia, Yemen, Aceh in Indonesia, and *Sharia* states in Nigeria. All of these countries have corporal punishment statutes.

In Islamic criminal justice systems, capital and corporal punishments are available for a variety of crimes. For instance, those who are deemed "Corrupt on earth" or those who committed major economic crimes with subversive intent are often sentenced to death, and the death penalty is available for victimless sexual crimes and religious crimes. Also, corporal punishment and other inhumane punishments are in practice in all Islamic criminal justice systems.

According to Muslim jurists, harsh punishments are imposable only if God has specifically, precisely, and clearly authorized such a punishment. Thus, support for the judicial corporal punishments found in Islamic texts should be clear and unambiguous. In classical Islamic law, corporal punishments such as flogging and amputation of body and organ retaliations are available under *qisas*, *tazir*, and *hudud* crimes.

Crime and Punishment in Islamic Criminal Justice Systems

Islamic law traditionally categorizes crimes according to the provenance of the authority to punish the offense. Islamic law recognizes four systems or categories for punishment. Under *had* or *hudud*, important crimes deemed to threaten the existence of Islam are punishable by penalties set by the Quran, or by the *Sunna* or *Sunnah* (tradition of Prophet Mohammad). Islamic jurists consider these sanctions immutable. They conclude that the judge is left with no discretion. *Hudud* punishments are to be prevented in case of doubt. This is based on the prophetic tradition which says: "Prevent the application of *hadd* punishment as much as you can whenever any doubt exists."[15] The standard of proof in *hodud* punishment is very high and difficult. It is recommended by *Sharia* law that judges should suggest the withdrawal of confession to an accused who has confessed to the commission of crime.[16] The infliction of the *hadd* punishment is restricted by repentance of the accused. For instance, if a thief repented and returned the stolen property before the application for prosecution is made, the *hadd* will lapse.[17]

The second system, *qisas*, concerns intentional crimes against the person. Its fundamental premise is the *lex talionis*, "eye for eye, tooth for tooth." *Lex talionis* is set out in the Quran, verse 5.32 (further developed by verse 17.33). The *lex talionis* appeared first in the Code of Hammurabi. It was a progressive penal reform, at that time aimed at enhancing the principle of proportionality. It is now seen as a basis for retribution. According to the Quran, the victim or his or her heirs are to inflict the punishment under the supervision of public authorities; the victims of such crimes may pardon the offender, in which case the death penalty or organ retaliation set by *qisas* will not be imposed.

Organ Retaliation (*qisas*) for injuries is prescribed in the Holy Quran: "We ordained therein for them, life for life, eye for eye, nose for nose, ear for ear, tooth for tooth and wounds equal to equal."[18] Conditions before *qisas* injuries are applicable:

(a) The injury must be deliberate and not accidental.
(b) The part of the body on which *qisas* may be inflicted must be the same, and in the same condition as the part of the victim's body which was injured by the culprit.
(c) *Qisas* must be practicable to inflict.[19]

In case the offender is pardoned by victims, two other systems of crime and punishment come into play. These are the *diyat* (prescribes restitution or compensation for the victim) and the *taazir* (public authorities set their own punishment, and the judge has wide discretion). Blood money (*diyat*) as compensation for victims of crimes prescribed by Holy Quran and tradition.[20] There is no corporal punishment under *diyats*.

Under the *taazir*, public authorities may provide for death penalty, corporal punishment, prison, or fine, but no religious text requires them to do so. The word *taazir* (discretionary punishment) means to prevent, to respect, and to reform. In the Islamic legal context, *taazir* is defined as follows: discretionary punishment to be delivered for transgressions against God, or against individuals for which there is neither fixed punishment nor penance. *Taazir* denotes a punishment aimed at the prevention of crime and reformation of the criminal. It is stated by Islamic scholars that the aim of *taazir* punishment is disciplinary, reformative, and deterrence.[21] *Taazir* punishment is not specified in either the Holy Quran or Sunnah of the Holy Prophet. Crimes for which there is no fixed punishment and concerning are left for the judge or the ruler to decide punishment and the manner of infliction (such as imprisonment, fine, and flogging less than prescribed punishments).[22]

In Islamic criminal justice systems, the legislature has approved corporal punishment in three different categories.

(1) *Prescribed Punishments (Hudud)*

- *Sodomy* is punishable by death if both the active and passive persons are mature, of sound mind, and have free will. If an adult male of legal capacity commits sexual intercourse with an immature person, the doer will be killed and the passive one will be subject to flogging under *taazir*. Number of lashes will be determined by the judge (please refer to table 5.1).
- *Adultery*: The Quran (24:2 Surah a Nur) only stipulates 100 lashes for adultery. When Prophet Mohammad stoned a number of men and women, and so this punishment is *Sharia*, Islamic law. But there is no historical evidence that this ever happened; there are two specific stories that are repeated, and in each the prophet required not only confession, but the culprits asked for their punishments.[23] In the case of fornication (when the perpetrators are unmarried), the punishment will be flogging.
- *Banditry* (*moharebeh or resorting to arms to frighten people*) is defined as an act of robbery by a group of armed men within the territory of the Islamic state that creates anarchy under which the property, privacy, safety, dignity, and religious values of the people would be violated. The crime is regarded as a war against God and his messenger. There are several alternative punishments for banditry, for instance execution, crucifixion, amputation of hand and foot, and exile (5:33, Surah Ma'ideh).
- *Apostasy* has an ambiguous basis in Islamic law. There is no reliable evidence that Prophet Mohammad executed anyone for this crime. However, the penalty for apostasy was common during the caliphate of Abu Bakr,

Table 5.1 Criminal Statute Prohibiting Sodomy in Iran

Crime	Citation	Punishment	Explanations
Sodomy	Sections 108–120 Islamic Penal Code of Iran	Death Penalty	*Sodomy is sexual intercourse between two men. *If a mature man of sound mind commits sexual intercourse with an immature person, the doer will be killed and the passive one will be subject to seventy-four lashes if not under duress. If an immature person commits sexual intercourse with another immature person, both of them will be subject to seventy-four lashes unless one of them is under duress.
Tafhiz (rubbing thighs or buttocks)	Sections 121–122 Islamic Penal Code of Iran	Flogging (100 lashes)	*When active person is non-Muslim and passive person is Muslim, punishment for passive person is death penalty. *If Tafhiz and the like are repeated three times without entry and punishment is enforced after each time, the punishment for the fourth time would be death.
Being naked under a cover	Section 123 Islamic Penal Code of Iran	Flogging (ninety-nine lashes)	*If two men not related by blood stand naked under one cover without any necessity.
Kissing	Section 124 Islamic Penal Code of Iran	Flogging (sixty lashes)	*If one man kisses another man with lust.

and there was a specific historical context that elicited the emergence of the law of apostasy.[24]

According to the US State Department, country human rights report, on October 14, 2019, Iranian authorities flogged Christian convert Mohammad Reza (Youhan) Omidi eighty times. A court had sentenced him to the flogging in 2016 for drinking wine as part of Holy Communion.

Capital and corporal punishments have been prescribed based on other *hudud* crimes as well.

In some circumstances recidivism will increase the punishment from flogging to a death sentence in Islamic criminal justice systems or the death penalty has been prescribed, mainly in the *Shiite* school of Islam:

- The punishment for *fornication* is flogging and after the fourth conviction the punishment is death, and the fornication of a non-Muslim with a Muslim female is a capital crime, as stated in the Holy Quran.
- *Lesbianism* (*mosaheqeh*) is female homosexuality. Punishment for lesbianism is one hundred (100) lashes for each party. Punishment for lesbianism is established vis-à-vis someone who is mature and of sound mind and has free will and intention. In *Sharia* law punishment for lesbianism, there is no distinction between the doer and the subject, as well as a Muslim or non-Muslim. If lesbianism is repeated three times and punishment is enforced each time, death sentence will be issued on the fourth conviction. For example, Article 131 of the former Islamic Penal Code of Iran provides that "if the act of lesbianism is repeated three times and punishment is enforced each time, death sentence will be issued the fourth time." The death penalty has been eliminated from the current Islamic Penal Code of Iran for this crime (for more information regarding lesbianism please refer to table 5.2).
- *False accusation of unlawful intercourse* (*qadhf*) is prohibited under *Sharia* law and it's punishable by flogging. Punishment for the fourth conviction is the death penalty. The rationale behind the Law of *qadhf* is here:
    (a) It serves as a protection for the generality of the Muslims. The law of the *qadhf* bans publishing people's unlawful connections and illicit relationships to the society.
    (b) To serve as a deterrent for the accuser and his like. When a person makes an allegation of adultery or fornication against someone and cannot prove his case, he should be punished for slander so that he might not slander in future.

Table 5.2 Criminal Statute Prohibiting Lesbianism in Iran

Crime	Citation	Punishment	Explanations
Lesbianism	Sections 127–133 Islamic Penal Code of Iran	Flogging (100 lashes)	***Lesbianism** (Mosaheqeh) is homosexuality of women by genitals. *In the punishment for lesbianism there will be no distinction between the doer and the subject as well as a Muslim or non-Muslim. *If the act of lesbianism is repeated three times and punishment is enforced each time, death sentence will be issued the fourth time.
Being naked under a cover	Section 134 Islamic Penal Code of Iran	Flogging (ninety-nine lashes)	*If two women not related by consanguinity stand naked under one cover without necessity, they will be punished with less than hundred (100) lashes. In case of its repetition as well as the repetition of punishment, hundred (100) lashes will be hit the third time.

- Punishment for the *had theft* is amputation of hand and after the fourth conviction it's death. Theft is defined in *Sharia* as the act of taking other people's property without any lawful claim to it. Theft deprives a man of property. It is an encroachment upon the property of man without any justifiable society and is looked upon with terror. Therefore, strict measures have been ordered by the Islamic criminal justice systems against thieves. The punishment for theft is in the Holy Quran: "As to the thief, male or female, cut off his or her hands as punishment by way of example from Allah for their crime. And Allah is exalted in power." According to a tradition of Prophet Mohammad, this punishment does not apply to petty larceny. However, the classical Islamic jurists differ as to the definition of petty larceny in terms of value of the stolen item. For instance, the Islamic Penal Code of Iran regulates sixteen different thefts, and just punishment for one category of theft is amputation. Punishment for nine categories of theft involves imprisonment and flogging.

In 2018, authorities in Mazandaran province of Iran amputated the hand of a man imprisoned for theft. According to a media report on May 23, 2018, prisoners convicted of theft and held at the Greater Tehran Prison were awaiting hand amputation. State media reported Attorney General Mohammad Jafar Montazeri stating he regretted that international pressure had caused an alleged drop in amputations in the countries with Islamic criminal justice system.

In January 2017, Amnesty International reported that authorities amputated the hand of a man sentenced for stealing livestock. The amputation by guillotine, which Amnesty characterized as "unspeakably cruel," took place at the central prison in Mashhad, Razavi Khorasan Province of Iran.

- Punishment for *wine drinking* during the time of the Holy Prophet was beating with shoes, sticks, and hands without specifying the number of lashes. In contemporary Islamic criminal justice systems, punishment for wine drinking is eighty lashes, and for the third conviction the death penalty will be imposed.

In August 2018, Amnesty International reported that authorities flogged Iranian singer and prisoner of conscience Peyman Mirzazadeh. According to the report, officials flogged Mirzazadeh 100 times for a conviction of drinking alcohol, and "insulting Islamic sanctities." The flogging, which Amnesty characterized as an "unspeakably cruel punishment," left Mirzazadeh in agonizing pain with a severely swollen back and legs.

(2) *Retaliation* (*qisas*) is imposed for *murder and organ retaliation*: The Quranic verses do not seem to require a nuanced inquiry into the circumstances of the murder before permitting the imposition of *qisas*. Classical Islamic law limited the death penalty and harsh corporal punishments for organ retaliation. It required a specific intent of the offender and granted certain family the right to override *qisas* by accepting *diyat* (blood money) or other compensation in lieu of the murderer's death or bodily injuries; also, classical Islamic law considered the status of the victim and offender.[25]

(3) *Discretionary punishments* (*taazir*): Discretionary punishments are the third category of punishments. Death penalty, corporal, prison, and fine are under this category. Islamic penal codes use *taazir* capital punishment for offenses such as: *defamation to sanctities*, *drug trafficking* in a specified amount, and for the *corruption on earth crimes*. Corruption on earth crimes have a vague definition. In Islamic criminal justice systems, corruption on earth is not a crime, and its definition can be attributed to crimes that include waging war against prophet and God, setting ablaze a mosque, destroying state property during internal rebellious, and any criticism of state.

Although the application of *hudud* is the right of God, and this made series of capital and corporal crimes an unalterable and unpardonable component of the Islamic criminal justice systems, the Muslim jurists have differed in their approach to the *hudud*. Disagreements are numerous, deep, and recurring. The first approach to be noted demands the immediate and strict application of *hudud*, assessing this as an essential prerequisite to truly defining a "Muslim majority society" as "Islamic."[26] According to a prominent Islamic scholar Mirza Ghomi,[27] while accepting the fact that the *hudud* is found in the textual references (the Quran and the tradition), considering the application of *hudud* to be based on the moves of the society must be just and, for some, has to be "ideal" before these injunctions could be applied. Thus, the priority is the promotion of social justice, fighting against poverty and illiteracy. Finally, there are others, also a minority, who consider the texts relating to *hudud* as obsolete and argue that these references have no place in contemporary Muslim societies.[28]

Despite the presence of the corporal punishments in Jewish and Islamic law sources, religion continues to be a powerful and variable resource for people of faith as they wrestle with the morality of bodily punishments. For instance, among those who opposed harsh punishments, 42% cited religion as their most important influence, while only 15% of those who favored harsh punishments said the same.[29]

Harsh Methods of Punishment in Islamic Criminal Justice Systems

Methods of judicial corporal punishments in Islamic criminal justice systems vary and can include flogging, amputation of hand for theft, cross amputation

(amputation of right hand and left leg) for *moharebeh,* and body mayhem for injuries. In some Islamic countries, public judicial corporal punishments are carried out to heighten the deterrent effect of punishment.

Methods of execution are harsh in Islamic criminal justice systems as well, and it can include hanging, shooting, beheading, stoning, and dropping the convict from a high wall. The *Mishnah*[30] mentions four methods of execution for a capital crime: stoning, burning, strangulation, and beheading.[31] Hanging as an execution method is not in practice in the Western countries. However, some Islamic countries routinely hang capital offenders. Many colonial-era penal codes, for instance, criminalized adultery and fornication and authorized judicial corporal punishment, but in contemporary time consensual homosexual acts have been decriminalized in most parts of the Western world. This profound clash of attitudes was not the result of some difference in degree of civilization. It was the result of differences in traditions of status.

Also, when the standards of society evolve, a society may come to the view that an act is not harmful and should no longer be criminalized. Even punishments that used to be traditional can become unusual when they fall out of use for a long time—usually for a century or more.[32] For example, whipping was an accepted form of judicial corporal punishment in the United States for two centuries and become disused, like the ducking stool or other forms of harsh judicial corporal punishments.[33]

The common method of execution in classical Islam was beheading by the sword, but in certain cases different methods are prescribed. For instance, in *Shiite* school, sodomy is punishable by beheading, stoning, burning, or dropping the convict from a high wall.[34] In some Muslim countries, governed by *Sharia* law, stoning is still practiced. Stoning as a form of punishment is provided in the criminal codes of the following Muslim countries: Iran, one province in Indonesia (Aceh), two federal states of Malaysia (Terengganu, Kelantan), twelve federal states in Northern Nigeria (Bauchi, Borno, Gombe, Jigawa, Kaduna, Kano, Katsina, Kebbi, Niger, Sokoto, Yobe, and Zamfara), Pakistan, Saudi Arabia, Sudan, and the United Arab Emirates.

In the Old Testament of the Bible, stoning is prescribed as the method of execution for crimes such as murder, blasphemy, or apostasy. The punishment of stoning to death (*rajm*) has a long tradition in Islam. When it comes to the practice of stoning adulterers, however, the traditions indicate that *Talmudic* law primarily influenced Mohammad. The *hadith* present Mohammad as initially prescribing stoning explicitly for Jews who had been found guilty of adultery then later referring to the Jewish law whenever he is passing similar sentences on members of his own community. Mohammad even criticized the Jews for relaxing their adultery laws when Jewish people replaced stoning with smearing of coal on the face.[35]

Punishment methods seem to be harsh in religious sources, but the punishment, the harshest in *Talmudic* law, was intended to be as quick and painless as possible given the nature of the punishment. Harsh Biblical penalties were carried out to the letter at one time, but certainly by *Mishnaic* times courts favored a lenient interpretation of the law. Considering the stones' size and execution conditions, the rabbis' ultimate concern was that the execution be as quick and as painless as possible, with minimal disfigurement. When one Rabbi suggested that the height of the platform should be increased so death by falling would be certain, another Rabbi responded that raising the platform is unacceptable, a fall from too high would result in disfigurement.[36] The punishment debate in the *Talmud*, therefore, can be viewed as not so much about justice, as about mercy. In the classic Jewish tradition, mercy occupies a central role.[37]

Avoidance of Harsh Punishments in Case of Doubt

Although harsh punishments have been prescribed in Jewish law, the *Talmud* seriously limits the use of harsh bodily punishments to criminals who were warned not to commit the crime in the presence of two witnesses and persisted in committing the crime also in front of two witnesses. In Jewish law a court of at least twenty-three judges would have to be satisfied, to a legal certainty, that the capital offense had been committed by the accused before the court could impose a death sentence. Since the testimony of two eyewitnesses was required, and the witnesses were subjected to searching and detailed interrogation by the court, there was rarely an instance when the evidence met the prescribed legal standard.[38]

Despite the scriptural mandate for capital and corporal punishments in Jewish law, two of the most influential sages of the second century of the first millennium, Rabbi Tarfon and Rabbi Akiva, stated that had they been in the *Sanhedrin* (the Supreme Court of ancient Israel) when Jews did have the political power to administer capital punishment in their community, no one would have ever been executed.[39] The *Gemara*[40] explains how they would preclude the death penalty without denying its divine legitimacy. The rabbis would ask improbable and obscure questions of the witnesses—such as whether it was not possible that the victim had been suffering from some fatal disease, which actually killed him. A lack of certainty by the witnesses on any material point would bar formal execution.[41]

Judicial corporal punishment does exist in Islamic textual references, and many Islamic countries and all Islamic nations with Islamic criminal justice system have these punishments in their penal codes. But it is possible to consider various evidentiary, procedural, and barriers against certain types of harsh judicial corporal punishments. These include the lack of a just and ideal religious criminal justice system for prosecution of *hudud* crimes.[42] Moreover, *avoidance of hudud crimes in case of doubt,*[43] more stringent evidentiary requirements, and pressures for twenty-first century norms of jurisprudence make implementation of the harsh punishments increasingly rare.

In Islamic criminal law, there is a principle that punishments are to be avoided whenever there is ambiguity or doubt as to the textual basis, evidence, or criminal culpability of the accused. In Islam, "*hudud* punishments are to be prevented in case of doubt." This is based on the prophetic tradition: "Prevent the application of *hadd* punishment as much as you can whenever any doubt exists." Shaykh Mufid[44] (*Shitte* jurist) notes that defective contracts give rise to *hudud* avoidance if entered into in the presence of doubt or ambiguity.[45] Also, Allameh Hilli[46] notes several types of *hadd*-averting doubt in one of his treatises.[47]

The standard of proof in *hudud* punishment is very high and difficult to attain. It is even recommended by the *Sharia* that a judge suggests the possibility of withdrawal of confession to an accused who has confessed to the commission of crime.[48]

Obviously, if these rules were followed in Islamic criminal justice systems, there would be almost no convictions in *hudud* capital cases. Unlike the contemporary practice of judicial corporal punishments in Islamic countries, both classical Islamic law and Jewish law have regarded barbarous punishments as totally unacceptable.

CONTEMPORARY USE OF CORPORAL PUNISHMENTS IN IRAN

How the Iranian Criminal Justice System Works?

Iran was ruled by monastic dynasties for over 2,500 years. *Shiism* became the official state religion under Safavid rule (1501–1722) and has been particularly influenced by the opinions of the sixth Imam, Abu Abdullah Jafar bin Mohammad Sadegh. Iran's legal school of thought is known as *Jafari* jurisprudence. According to the *Jafari* school, sources of Islamic law are the Holy Quran, tradition (*hadith*), the consensus of the jurist (*ijma*), and reason (*'aql*). The increasing influence of foreign powers in the region under the Qajars (1795–1925) began with a series of capitulations to Europeans, beginning with the Russians, in the nineteenth century.[49] In 1906, the first Iranian Constitution was written. A series of laws were subsequently enacted relating to criminal, civil, commercial, and family law. The first Penal Code of Iran was ratified in 1926.[50]

Iran's secular criminal justice system was formed under the Pahlavi Dynasty (1925–1979) and its two monarchs, Reza Shah (1925–1941) and

Mohammad Reza Shah (*Aryamehr*; 1941–1979). Its modern criminal law is based on modern capitalist notions of crime and punishment. By 1936, Iranian legislation made secular education a requisite for serving judges.[51] The 1979 Islamic Revolution brought an end to the Pahlavi Dynasty. The Iranian Supreme Judicial Council issued a proclamation directing all courts that all non-Islamic legislation be suspended. The council revised all laws so that they would conform to an Islamic legal system, with Ayatollah Rohollah Mosavi Khomeini's *fatawa* serving as transitional laws. The punishment system in Iran is now based on the Twelve *Imami Shii* version of *Sharia* law, which was formed in the early 1980s, during the tenure of the Ayatollah Khomeini.[52] In Iran after the Islamic Revolution, the state's concept of justice derived from the religious principles of Islam, in which *Sharia*—the general and particular rules of Islamic *corpus juris*—is not just a code of law but a code of conduct of behavior and ethics, an inseparable combination of law and morality.

Evidence of the relationship of the state to an Islamic concept of justice can be seen in the Penal Code of Iran. In 1983, the Statute of Retaliation and Prescribed Punishments was ratified. This Statute allows capital and corporal punishments for crimes outlined in the Holy Quran and tradition. For other crimes, jurists still refer to the modern Penal Code of Iran. In 1984, the Discretionary Punishment Statute was ratified. Chapters 2 and 3 of the Islamic Penal Code, which was ratified in 1992, concern retaliation and prescribed punishments. Chapter 5 of the Islamic Penal Code was ratified in 1997. Chapter 5 was developed to deal with discretionary and preventive punishments.[53] The Islamic Penal Code provides the death penalty for more than fifteen crimes and corporal punishments such as flogging, organ retaliation, and mutilation of body for variety of crimes. Furthermore, Article 729 of the Islamic Penal Code abolishes all contrary statutes, including the modern Penal Code of Iran. Finally, in 2013, Iran ratified a new Islamic Penal Code with a series of changes. The recent Islamic Penal Code of Iran has expanded the use of alternatives to imprisonment.

The contemporary Islamic criminal justice system of Iran categorizes crimes and punishments according to the provenance of the authority to punish the offense. The Islamic Penal Code of Iran recognizes five systems or categories for crimes and punishments: prescribed punishments (*hadd* or *hudud*), retaliation (*qisas*), blood money (*diyat*), prescribed punishments (*taazir*), and preventive punishments (*mojazathayeh bazdarandeh*). In Iran, the sanction for prescribed punishment in many cases is corporal punishment. *Hadd* punishment includes flogging and mutilation. Because *hadd* is the principal punishment in Iran, there is no alternative sanction for prescribed punishments.[54] Preventive punishment is prescribed by the Iranian government in order to protect order and compliance with governmental regulations.[55]

Examples include imprisonment and fines. There is no corporal punishment under preventive punishments.

In addition to the death penalty and corporal punishments such as flogging and body mutilation, the contemporary Iranian criminal justice system also provides for imprisonment, fines, *diya* (blood money restitution to victims), probation and parole, and community service.

Based on Iran's Penal Code before the Islamic Revolution, in addition to murder, the death penalty was used to punish drug trafficking and offenses against public securities. In the former Penal Code of Iran, the death penalty was applied for specific crimes. After the Islamic Revolution, the application of the death penalty was expanded. The death penalty in Iran is applicable to an overly broad range of crimes in addition to murder, including incest, rape, sex between a non-Muslim and a Muslim female, adultery, sodomy, other homosexual acts after fourth conviction, drinking liquor after three convictions, drawing arms to create fear, defamation to what is holy, drug trafficking in special amounts, corruption on earth, fornication upon a fourth conviction, false accusation of unlawful intercourse upon a fourth conviction, and *hadd* theft.[56]

Under the Iranian criminal justice system, execution may be conducted in public to enhance its alleged effect of general deterrence. There is no open indication regarding public punishments in the penal system of Iran. Public hangings and flogging are normally carried out sparingly in Iran and reserved for cases that have provoked public outrage, such as serial murders, sexual crimes or child killings. Based on the regulation regarding the execution methods of retaliation sentences, "if the presence of viewers or other people during the execution is not advisable, with district attorney instruction, police may prevent the public from the execution scene."[57]

Corporal punishment is the punishment of body. It is defined as physical punishment as distinguished from pecuniary punishment or a fine, or any kind of punishment of or inflicted on the body.[58] Following the reign of the Pahlavi monarchs flogging was imposed for three crimes. Based on modern Iran's Penal Code the only applicable corporal punishment was flogging for knife-stabbing,[59] vagrancy,[60] and gaining ownership of another person's property.[61] In 1966, Iran's parliament ratified the Abolition of Flogging Statute, and flogging was abolished in Iran in 1966.[62] However, with Islamic government approval, flogging is now permitted in Iran for various crimes, as indicated in figure 4.1 in chapter 4.

Another difference in the Iranian criminal justice system is criminalization of status crimes. Offenses have traditionally been defined in terms of acts or failure to act.[63] Despite the general rule that in order to be considered a crime, an act must be one that is prohibited or recognized as a failure to act, certain atypical offenses are defined in terms of personal status or condition of being rather than in terms of the acts committed—for example, being a vagrant, prostitute, drunkard, gambler, beggar, narcotic addict, or homosexual. The more recent tendency in the law is to hold people criminally culpable only for specific acts.[64] For example, in Iran drug addiction as a status has been considered a crime. In Iran, first-time offenses for drug addicts carry a sentence from five hundred thousand rials to one million rials and four to twelve months of imprisonment. A second offense is punishable with a cash fine of one million rials to four million rials and one to three years of imprisonment. For government employees, the sentences are harsher: in addition to the cash fine and imprisonment, they shall be permanently dismissed from government office. The sentence is multiplied for the third and any other subsequent offense: it increases the second offense by two- to fourfold, plus fifty lashes. The same punishments apply to offenders who are offered treatment in rehabilitation centers.[65]

Also, unlike the United States, vagrancy is punishable in Iran. There is no implicit definition of what constitutes vagrancy in Iran. In the United States, some jurisdictions have repealed such traditional statutes in favor of laws prohibiting specific conduct and making no use of the term "vagrancy" or "vagrant." However, the mere fact that a statute prohibits specific conduct and eschews the terms vagrancy and vagrant does not make it proof against a challenge on vagueness grounds.

Different Types of Corporal Punishments

The Iranian criminal justice system has approved three types of corporal punishment: flogging, organ retaliation, and punitive amputation.

a) *Flogging*: The punishment for the following crimes have been indicated in Quran or tradition of Prophet Mohammad:

—The punishment of *fornication* is 100 lashes as stated in the Holy Quran.[66]

—*Sodomy* entails execution if both the active and passive persons are mature, of sound mind, and have free will. If a mature man of sound mind commits sexual intercourse with an immature person, the doer will be killed and the passive one will be subject to *taazir* (Discretionary punishment awarded by the judge) of seventy-four lashes if not under duress. When the active person is non-Muslim, and the passive person is Muslim punishment for the passive person is death penalty. If an immature person commits sexual intercourse with another minor, both will be subject to *taazir* (seventy-four lashes) unless one was under duress.[67]

—*Lesbianism* (*mosaheqeh*) is homosexuality of women by genitals. Punishment for lesbianism is one hundred (100) lashes. Punishment for lesbianism will be established vis-à-vis someone who is mature, of sound mind, and has free will and intention. Punishment for lesbianism makes no distinction between the doer and the subject as well as a Muslim or non-Muslim. If the act of lesbianism is repeated three times and punishment is enforced each time, the death sentence will be issued the fourth time.[68]

—*False accusation of unlawful intercourse*[69] is prohibited under Islamic Penal Code by 80 lashes.

—Punishment for *wine drinking* during the time of Holy Prophet was public beating with shoes, sticks, and hands without specifying the number of lashes.[70] Under the Islamic Penal Code of Iran, the punishment for wine drinking is eighty lashes.[71]

The Islamic Penal Code of Iran considered flogging as a discretionary punishment for different crimes as a principal punishment, or as a voluntary principal punishment. In these cases, judges can sentence flogging or fine/flogging or imprisonment. As to whether *taazir* punishment may exceed the *hadd* punishment, there is a prophet tradition which says: "The man who shall inflict scourging, to the amount of punishment in case where *hadd* is not established shall be counted an aggravator."[72] (For more information regarding corporal punishment in Quran, refer to table 5.3.)

b) *Organ Retaliation* (*qisas*):

Qisas is explained as follows in Article 269 of the Islamic Penal Code: "cutting off bodily organ or its injury if it were to be intentional is subject to

Table 5.3 Corporal Punishment in the Quran and Tradition

Crime category	Punishment in the Quran	Punishment in the tradition
Maiming	Retaliation in kind or monetary restitution	Monetary restitution based on authentic tradition
False accusation of unlawful intercourse	Public flogging	Different tradition
Resorting to arms in order to frighten people	Crucifixion or amputation of alternate hand and foot	Different tradition
Thievery	Amputation of four fingers	Amputation of four fingers based on tradition
Adultery	Public flogging of the two parties involved in adultery	Different tradition
Sodomy	Public flogging	Different tradition
Wine drinking	Public flogging	Different tradition
Lesbianism	Public flogging	Different tradition
False witness	Public flogging	Different tradition

retaliation in kind and the wronged party is allowed for retaliation against the criminal based on the prescribed norms and religious judge's decree." Article 271 defines three types of intentional cutting or injury as follows: (a) when the criminal intends to inflict such a cut and/or injury by the commission of a certain act whether the acts result to inflict such a cut and/or injury; (b) when the criminal intentionally commits an act that somewhat results in a cut and/or injury although this was not intended to cut and/or injure; and (c) when the criminal does not intend to cut or injure an organ, and his act does not effectuate that result, but, due to the advanced age and/or infancy, the act effectuates the severance or injury of organs and it is known to the criminal. But by providing equity conditions in the health of organs, in originality of organs, in the place of injury, the retaliation is not fatal, and it is not more injurious than the crime,[73] the legislature goal in Iran is to restrict the application of organ retaliation. Therefore, judges in the majority of cases convert *qisas* sentences to that of imprisonment.

c) Punitive amputation:

—*Theft* is an act of taking other people's property without any lawful claim to it. The following punishment for theft is prescribed in the Holy Quran: "As to the thief, male or female, cut off his or her hands as punishment by way of example from Allah for their crime. And Allah is exalted in power."[74] According to a tradition of Prophet Mohammad, this harsh punishment does not apply to petty larceny. However, the classical jurists differ as to the definition of petty larceny in terms of value of the property stolen. For this reason, under Islamic Penal Code sixteen different thefts are regulated. Just punishment for one type of theft—with specific restrictions—is amputation. Punishment for nine types of thefts is both imprisonment and flogging.[75] For the *had* theft to be punishable by amputation in the Iranian criminal justice system, the following conditions must be proven: puberty and sanity of the thief, there was no threat or coercion for the commission of theft, the act of theft is willful, knowledge of the defendant that property belongs to another person, knowledge of the defendant that the act of theft is a crime, property should be located in the safe custody, breaking and entering, the minimum value of property, lack of necessity, thief is not the father of the owner, safe custody did not belong to the thief previously, the act is stealing, lack of famine in community, proportionate safe custody, and stolen goods are not government property of unknown ownership.

—*Moharebeh* (*Resorting to arms in order to frighten people*) is defined as an act of robbery by a group of armed men within the territory of the Islamic state so as to create anarchy under which the property, privacy, safety, dignity, and religious values of the people would be violated. The crime is regarded as a war against God and his messenger. Corruption on earth crime has a vague definition in Iranian criminal justice system.

> Corruption on earth is not a crime. It can be attributed to any act including waging against prophet and God, setting ablaze a mosque, destroying state during internal rebellion, and any criticism of state (crimes against public order). There are several alternative punishments, that is, execution, crucifixion, amputation of hand and foot, and exile. Therefore, it is open to judge to pass any one of these sentences which he thinks fit under the circumstances of each case.[76]

In total, more than twenty-seven crimes are punishable by flogging under the Iranian criminal justice system. Although, one special type of theft (*hadd* theft) and "resorting to arms in order to frighten people" (*moharebeh)* might be punishable by amputation and organ retaliation is an alternative punishment for body injuries, in practice the use of amputation and organ retaliation as a form of punishment is very rare in Iran.

In 2021, at least 152 people were sentenced to flogging,[77] and in 2020 at least 160 people were sentenced to flogging, according to the Abdorrahman Boroumand Center, for theft and assault as well as for acts that are protected under international human rights law, such as participating in peaceful protests, engaging in extramarital or consensual same-sex relationships, and attending mixed-gender parties. In many cases, flogging sentences were carried out.

Judicially sanctioned corporal punishments are common in Iran. These included flogging, blinding, and amputation, which the government defends as "punishment" and does not consider to be torture.[78] According to the Abdorrahman Boroumand Foundation, between January 1 and September 2 of 2021, Iranian authorities sentenced at least seventy-seven individuals to amputation and carried out these sentences in at least eight cases. There were no official recorded cases of amputation during the year.

> According to Amnesty International, authorities flogged Hadi Rostami, an inmate at Orumiyeh Prison in West Azerbaijan Province, sixty times on February 14 for "disrupting prison order." Extrajudicial punishments by authorities involving degrading public humiliation of alleged offenders were also frequently reported throughout the year. Authorities regularly forced alleged offenders to make videotaped confessions that the government later televised. In another recent case of flogging, Hadi Atazadeh died in Ahar prison of Iran in September 2021 after being flogged.

Harshness of Iranian Criminal Justice System

Harshness of criminal justice systems and social reactions about it is complex, and the history of harsh punishment is linked to various patterns in human social development. Harshness of the Iranian criminal justice system depends on how different social traditions have emerged. Therefore, harshness and mildness of a punishment are completely different from culture to culture and from era to era. For instance, flogging which is a harsh punishment in the Western countries, in Islamic penal system is regarded as a mild one, or while branding was a mild punishment in ancient era, in the twenty-first century it is regarded as a harsh punishment.

Therefore, cultural factors are important in evaluating whether punishment is cruel and unusual. Factors of penal harshness will depend on a number of personal elements that are socially conditioned. For example, in *Tyrer v. United Kingdom* the continental judges of the European Court of Human Rights were shocked at the practice of birching, but Judge Gerald Fitzmaurice was not at all outraged. Because he was educated under a system according to which the corporal punishment of schoolboys was regarded as the normal sanction for serious or even less serious misbehavior. But there must be a limit to the role cultural factors may play. Otherwise, the norm prohibiting cruel and unusual punishment ceases to have any international scope. Although a "margin of appreciation" in applying fundamental rights is recognized within the European system, such bodies as the Human Rights Committee and the Committee against Torture have yet to elaborate a doctrine on just how broadly cultural factors may be invoked within the context of cruel treatment and torture.[79]

Since Montesquieu,[80] people have believed that harsh punishment is produced by strong states, with relatively unbridled power. Durkheim[81] stated it as nothing less than a law: The intensity of punishment, he held, depended not only on the complexity of a society but on the absolute character of its state power.[82]

Harsh criminal punishment has an overwhelming impact on a convict's life. Criminal punishment represents government at its most coercive. For affected individuals, the stakes are much higher with respect to other forms of governmental regulation. Criminal punishment may deprive a person of physical liberty for decades, and even of life itself.[83]

The common understanding of a "cruel" punishment is one that is unnecessarily harsh. But a punishment may be unnecessarily harsh for one purpose but not for another. For instance, in the twenty-first century, ten years imprisonment at hard labor would be gratuitously harsh and therefore "cruel" for a libel offense, but not for murder. The same may be said of the term "unusual." For example, life imprisonment for a minor shoplifting is unusual, but life sentences for other offenses involving more aggravated culpability or harms such as kidnapping are usual.

Thus, what constitutes cruelty differs from one society to another. For instance, the European Court of Human Rights considered whether corporal punishment by birching violates "inhuman or degrading treatment or

Punishment," Judge Fitzmaurice, who sat on behalf of the United Kingdom, admitted that in his view there was no violation undoubtedly one to be conditioned by his own youthful experience in English Public schools. His views were not shared by the majority of the court, perhaps because the other judges could not empathize with his nostalgia for such brutality and had not been culturally conditioned to appreciate its alleged benefits.[84]

Respectful modes of punishment, for conception of humanity, can ground a more humane penal system.[85] But the respectful treatment is dramatically absent in the Iranian penal systems in contrast with International Conventions.[86] How can a country that rhetorically portrays itself as one of the oldest civilizations maintain punitive practices that are so much harsher than in the majority of states? Punishments in the Islamic criminal justice system of Iran are harsh. What is going on in the penal system of Iran? How have the cultural roots of harsh punishment emerged in contemporary Iran? How harsh criminal punishments can develop in a society that has old cultural roots?

These questions are left aside by contemporary sociological theorists. They often talk in general terms about "modernity" and "post-modernity" but may not attend to such differences between countries, and by philosophers whose abstract theorizing about "the justification of punishment, and about such issues as proportionality, fails to attend to those more particular, substantive features of penalty that distinguish penal systems from each other and that are so central to the reality and meaning of criminal punishment."

We can consider the following factors to find out if the Iranian criminal justice system is harsh:

1. Harshness in criminalizing conduct: A criminal justice system that criminalizes more moral offenses and has more crimes in its penal code is harsher than one that criminalizes few moral offenses.[87] The Iranian criminal justice system has criminalized several consensual sexual acts and has variety of capital crimes.
2. Harshness in subjecting numerous classes of persons to potential criminal liability:[88] A criminal justice system that prosecutes juveniles as adults can be called harsher than a system that treats them as juveniles. The Iranian criminal justice system executes juveniles. Also, nine-year-old girls and fifteen-year-old boys are fully criminally liable under the Islamic criminal justice system of Iran.
3. Harshness in grading: If two systems both treat possession of narcotics as an offense, but one system grades it as a felony and another system as a misdemeanor, the first system is harsher.[89] In the Iranian criminal justice system, possession of narcotic can be a capital crime.
4. Harshness in inflexible doctrines of criminal liability:[90] When the definition of self-defense is narrower in Iran compared to the United States,

the Iranian criminal justice system is harsher compared to American criminal justice system.

5. Harshness in enforcement: When in the Iranian criminal justice system police routinely ignore violations of law compared to a criminal justice system that let few offenses go unpunished, the Iranian criminal justice system is mild in this regard.
6. Harshness in the law of punishment:[91] When the Iranian criminal justice system uses severe punishments such as death penalty, flogging, mutilation of body. and long-term imprisonment, it shows the Islamic penal system of Iran is harsher compared to countries that have abolished capital and corporal punishments.
7. Harshness in the application of punishment:[92] This is the way officials administer punishment. When Iranian judges sentence capital offenders to hanging or stoning, the criminal justice system of Iran is harsher compared to a system that has lethal injection as a method of execution.
8. Harshness in the inflexibility of punishment: A system that does not consider individualization and treats all offenders equally severely is a harsh system.[93] Based on the Islamic Penal Code of Iran since certain Islamic punishments are mandatory, the judges cannot apply aggravating and mitigating factors in *hodoud* and *qisas* punishments.

To bolster these hypotheses that the punishments in Iran are harsh, status criminalized in the United States includes some high-level sex or morals offenses,[94] and some sex offenses have been decriminalized,[95] but in Iran status statutes include sex and moral offenses,[96] vagrancy,[97] drunkenness,[98] and addiction.[99]

Europe, on the other hand, has decriminalized or even legalized an increasing number of morals offenses, such as prostitution and drug offenses. Most Europeans are familiar with the liberal Dutch policies pertaining to cannabis and the legalization of prostitution.[100]

Different forms of punishment provisions threatening long prison terms for drug offenders, and recidivists have led to an unprecedented growth in the prison population.

Even though the desire for punitiveness in Iran may not be as diametrically different as current penal policies indicate, the types of discourse diverge dramatically. In Iran, arguments pertaining to the inherent dignity or human rights of individual offenders have fallen on deaf ears, and the law frequently affirms this attitude. In Iran, even some particularly Islamic provisions have successfully asserted dignity rights, but not necessarily in the Islamic criminal justice system.

It is obvious that social and political hierarchies have led to mild punishments while a weak state, violence in history or religious beliefs, and egalitarianism have caused more degrading and harsh punishment in Iran and other Islamic criminal justice systems.

In order to determine whether a punishment is cruel and unusual, it is necessary to inquire into the extent the punishment deprives the offender of life, liberty, or property. Five objectives that may be achieved by the imposition of criminal sanctions: deterrence, retribution, rehabilitation, incapacitation, and expression of society's condemnation. Moreover, are these goals observable in the harsh system of punishment or mild?

Evolving standards of decency preclude inflictions of pain without penological justification because these would fall in the category of unnecessary and wanton inflictions of pain.[101] The severe pain resulting from the punishments can be justified as having a deterrent impact. Even small gains in deterrence can be defended as necessary to prevent serious crimes. Such claims are absurd. In Iran after the revolutionary restatement of Islamic punishments, such criminal sanctions were justified on precisely this ground. But a claim that cruel punishment such as corporal punishment deters high crime rates might be in error.

Accordingly, the ordinary European view is that the role of retributivism must be strictly limited, and punishment professionals remain quite attached to rehabilitationist programs.[102] Of course, there are no such limits in Iran.

As Bentham[103] indicates, "legislators and men in general are naturally inclined" to extreme harshness, since "antipathy, or a want of compassion for individuals who are represented as dangerous and vile, pushes them onward to an undue severity."[104] Criminal punishment does not only visit measured retribution on blameworthy offenders. Nor does it only deter. Nor does it only express considered condemnation.

The choice of rehabilitation for the criminal justice system is indeed the choice of a system that treats offenders as inferiors and also some measure of indulgence and even kindness. In practice, the choice for retributivism is turning out to be the choice, not for equality, but for degradation.[105]

Regarding incapacitation, restricting the use of predictions of dangerousness in sentencing decisions itself safeguards against overly harsh punishment. We are less likely to endorse excessive criminal sanctions if we truly consider ourselves at risk of having the harsher sanctions apply to us. Conversely, the perception that only predictably dangerous persons are at risk of the harsher sentences, combined with a rare perception of ourselves as one of the predictably dangerous, will tend to render us more receptive to extending the higher end of the range of available sentences.[106]

An adequate definition of harsh punishment must focus on both punishment's objective effects and the punisher's culpability.[107] Imagine for a moment that the focus is solely on objective effects. In this view, a punishment is harsh if it does not promote a legitimate penological objective in point of fact. It does not matter that the punisher believes, even reasonably so, that the punishment has redeeming value.

The disqualifying problem with an exclusive focus on objective effects is that it does not give the punisher the required decision.[108] Sometimes explicitly and other times implicitly, it has required the punisher to possess culpability respecting a punishment's lack of redeeming value. As a general matter, the objective reasonableness standard covering the appropriate balance between respecting the decisional discretion of legislatures and other actors, on the one hand, and avoiding intrusive state-of-mind inquiries and imposing insurmountable evidentiary burdens, on the other.[109]

In short, we can define a harsh punishment as one that, first, does not promote a legitimate penological goal as a matter of objective reality and, second, is either not believed to have redeeming value by those authorizing or inflicting the punishment or is recklessly or negligently believed to have such value.

NOTES

1. 5:38 Quran.
2. Country Report on Corporal Punishment, *End Corporal Punishment,* from: https://endcorporalpunishment.org/reports-on-every-state-and-territory/.
3. In United States still shame punishments are available and bills that have proposed whipping as a punishment.
4. Daniel Hall, *When Canning Meets the Eighth Amendment: Whipping Offenders in the United States*, 4 Widenr J. Pub. L. 403 (1995).
5. Judicial corporal punishment.
6. John Gleissner, *Prison Overcrowding Cure: Judicial Corporal Punishment of Adults*, 49 Criminal Law Bulletin (4), 2 (2013).
7. H.R. 1077, Legis. Sess., 1995 Md. Laws; H.R. 106, Reg. Sess., 1995 Miss. Laws.
8. H.R. 106, Reg. Sess., 1995 Miss. Laws.
9. Ann O'Hanlon, *New Interest in Corporal Punishment*, Wash. Post, Mar. 5, 1995, at A21 (explaining that although California's paddling bill did not pass, it was reintroduced by Assemblyman Mickey Conroy in February, 1995).
10. See *Singapore to Cane Second Foreigner for Vandalism*, Reuters Info. Services, Apr. 22, 1994, available in LEXIS, World Library, Allwld File (acknowledging worldwide controversy over the justifications for caning).
11. Ronald Brownstein, Singapore's Caning Sentence Divides Americans, Poll Finds, Los Angeles Times, April 1994. From https://www.latimes.com/archives/la-xpm-1994-04-21-mn-48524-story.html.
12. Kenneth Shuster, *Halacha as a Model for American Penal Practice: A Comparison of Halachic and American Punishment Methods*, 19 Nova L. Rev. 965 (1995).

13. *Id.*
14. Cherif Bassiouni, *Introduction to Islam* (Rand McNally & Company, 1988).
15. Mohammad Bahrami, *Islamic Jurisprudence and Legal Analysis of Hodoud punishments are to be prevented in case of doubt*, 5 Legal viewpoints Journal (1376 Solar Hejira) [In Farsi].
16. *Id.*
17. Islamic Penal Code of Iran, Art 198/4 (1991) [In Farsi].
18. Holy Quran, Maedeh Surah, 45 Verse.
19. See Islamic Penal Code of Iran, Art 271–272.
20. *Id,* Art 15.
21. Matthew Lippman, Sean McConville, and Mordechai Yerushalmi, *Islamic Criminal Law and Procedure: An Introduction* (New York: Praeger publication, 1988).
22. See Islamic Penal Code of Iran, Art 498–729.
23. Eesa Ebrahimi., *Philosophy of Punishment in Islam,* 36, 38, Bar Association Journal, Tehran (1333 Solar Hejira) [In Farsi].
24. Emily Ownes, *Religion and the Death Penalty* (William Eerdmans Publishing company, 2004).
25. Anderson, J.N.D. *Homicide in Islamic Law*, 13 Bulletin of the School of Oriental & African Stud. 811, 815 (1951).
26. Hossein Ali, Montazeri, *Tozihol al-masayel* (Fekr Publication: Tehran, Iran, 1998).
27. Mirza Ghomi, *Jame al-shetat (Vol, 1),* Keyhan Publication (1992).
28. Tariq Ramadan, *New Directions in Islamic Thought: Exploring Reform and Muslim Tradition,* I.B. Tauris & Co. Ltd (2009).
29. Emily Ownes, *supra* note 24.
30. Mishna is the first major written collection of the Jewish oral traditions which is known as the Oral Torah.
31. Mishnah, Sanhedrin 49b–50b.
32. John F. Stinneford, *The Original Meaning of "Cruel."* 105 GEO. L.J. 441, 443 (2017).
33. Merin Cherian, *Cruel, Unusual, and Unconstitutional: An Originalist Argument for Ending Long-Term Solitary Confinement.* 56 Am. Crim. L. Rev. (2019): 1759.
34. Rudolph Peters, *Crime and Punishment in Islamic Law,* 36 (Cambridge University Press, 2006).
35. A hadith recorded by al-Bukhari, on the authority of ibn Umar states: A Jew and a Jewess were brought to Allah's Apostle (S) on a charge of committing illegal sexual intercourse. The Prophet asked them: "What is the legal punishment (for this sin) in your Book (Torah)?" They replied: "Our priests have innovated the blackening of faces with charcoal and Tajbiya" (being mounted on a donkey, with their faces in opposite directions, then mortified in public). Abdullah bin Salaam said: "O Allah's Apostle, tell them to bring the Torah." The Torah was brought, and then one of the Jews put his hand over the Divine Verse of the *rajm* (stoning to death) and started reading what preceded and what followed it. On that, Ibn Salaam said to the Jew:

"Lift up your hand." The Divine Verse of the *rajm* was under his hand. So, Allah's Apostle (S) ordered that the two (sinners) be stoned to death, and so they were stoned.

36. Sanaz Alasti, Comparative study of stoning punishment in the religions of Islam and Judaism, *Justice Policy Journal* 4, no. 1–38 (2007).

37. Bruce S. Ledewitz, and Scott Staples, *Reflections on the Talmudic and American Death Penalty*, 6 U. Fla. JL & Pub. Pol'y, 33 (1993).

38. See Maimonides, Mishneh Torah, Book of Judges, Sanhedrin, chapter XII.

39. Mishnah: Makkot 1.10.

40. The second part of the Talmud, consisting primarily rabbinical analysis of and commentary on the Mishnah.

41. Ledewitz, *supra* note 37.

42. Mirza Ghomi, *Jama al-Shetat, supra* note 27.

43. This Islamic legal maxim says that judges are to avoid imposing *hudud* punishments when beset by doubts as to the scope of the law or the sufficiency of the evidence.

44. Abu 'Abd Allah Muhammad ibn Muhammad ibn al-Nu'man al-'Ukbari al-Baghdadi known as Shaykh Mufid for his expertise in philosophical theology (c. 948–1022 CE) was an eminent Twelver Shi'a theologian.

45. Mufid, *Muqni'ah* (Qom, Iran: Mu'assasat Nashr Islami, 1410/[1990]), 789 [In Arabic].

46. Hassan bin Sadid-Aldin (Allameh Hilli) was born on 29th Ramadan of 648 A.H. He learned knowledge and philosophy from famous Iranian scientist of seventh century "Khajeh Nasireddin-e Tousi." He was an eminent Twelver theologian who flourished under the Mongols in Iraq.

47. Allameh Hilli, *Qawa'id al-ahkam* (Qom, Iran: Mu'assasat Nashr Islami, 1413–1419/ [1992-1999]), 3:521–523 [In Arabic].

48. Sanaz Alasti, *supra* note 36.

49. Hassan Amin, *The History of Law in Iran*, 12 (Encyclopedia of Iran, 2004).

50. Sanaz Alasti and Eric Bronson, Crime and Punishment in Iran (Islamic Republic of), *The Encyclopedia of Crime and Punishment*, 1–5 (Wiley-Blackwell, 2015).

51. Sanaz Alasti, *Cruel and Unusual Punishment: Comparative Perspective in International Conventions, the United States and Iran*, 57 (Florida: Vandeplas, 2008).

52. *Id, at* 58.

53. Iraj Goldouzian, *Special Criminal Law* (Iran, Tehran: Mizan Publication, 2001) [In Farsi].

54. See Islamic Penal Code of Iran.

55. *Id,* Art 17.

56. Islamic Penal Code of Iran (2013).

57. Sanaz Alasti and Eric Bronson, *supra* note 50.

58. Steven A. Hatfield, *Criminal Punishment in America: From the Colonial to the Modern Era*, 1 USAFA J. Leg. Stud. 180 (1990).

59. General Penal Code of Iran, Art. 173 (1923). [In Farsi]

60. General Penal Code of Iran, Art. 273.

61. Statute Regarding the Transferring of Property, Art 3 (1923). [In Farsi]

62. Abolition of Flogging Statute, Single Clause (1966). [In Farsi]

63. Forrest Lacey, *Vagrancy and Other Crimes of Personal Condition,* Harvard Law Review 66 (1953).
64. *American Jurisprudence* (2nd ed.), vol. 21., Criminal Laws, 31.
65. Anti Narcotic Drugs Statute, Arts. 16 and 17 (1989).
66. Holy Quran, Soreh Noor, 2 verse.
67. Islamic Penal Code of Iran, Art. 110-113, 121.
68. *Id,* Art. 127, 129, 130, 131.
69. *Id,* Art 139.
70. Lippman, *supra* note 21.
71. Islamic Penal Code of Iran, Art 174.
72. Lippman, *supra* note 21.
73. Islamic Penal Code of Iran, Art 272.
74. Holy Quran, *Soreh Maedeh*, 38 verse.
75. Islamic Penal Code of Iran, Art 651–667.
76. Abolghasem Gorji, *Legal Injunctions of the Quran*, 186–188 (Iran, Tehran: Mizan Publication, 2004).
77. Amnesty International Report 2021/2022: The State of the World's Human Rights Report (2022).
78. US Department of State, Country Reports on Human Rights (2021).
79. William A. Schabas, *The Death Penalty as Cruel Treatment and Torture*, 51–52 (Northeastern University Press, 1996).
80. Montesquieu was one of the great political philosophers of the Enlightenment. He constructed a naturalistic account of the various forms of government, and of the causes that made them what they were and that advanced or constrained their development. He used this account to explain how governments might be preserved from corruption. He saw despotism, in particular, as a standing danger for any government not already despotic and argued that it could best be prevented by a system in which different bodies exercised legislative, executive, and judicial power, and in which all those bodies were bound by the rule of law. This theory of the separation of powers had an enormous impact on liberal political theory, and on the framers of the constitution of the United States of America.
81. Émile Durkheim was a French sociologist who rose to prominence in the late nineteenth and early twentieth centuries. Along with Karl Marx and Max Weber, he is credited as being one of the principal founders of modern sociology.
82. Durkheim, *Two Laws of Penal Evolution, 21, in M. Gane, ed.* (London: The Radical Sociology of Durkheim and Mauss, 1992).
83. Tom Stacy, *Cleaning up the Eighth Amendment Mess,* 14 Wm. & Mary Bill Rts. J. 475 (December 2005).
84. *Id.*
85. R.A. Duff, *Punishment, Dignity and Degradation,* 25 Oxford J. Legal Stud. 141 (Spring 2005).
86. Sanaz Alasti, supra note 51, at 43.
87. James Whiteman, *Harsh Justice: Criminal Punishment and the Widening divide between America and Europe,* 33 (New York: Oxford University Press, 2003).

88. *Id.*, 34.
89. *Id.*
90. *Id.*, 35.
91. *Id.*
92. *Id.*
93. *Id.*
94. *Id*, 43–45.
95. R.A. Duff, *supra* note 85.
96. Islamic Penal Code of Iran, Art 221-261, 2013 [In Farsi].
97. *Id*, Art 712, 2013 [In Farsi].
98. *Id*, Art 264–266, 2013 [In Farsi].
99. Anti-Narcotics Drug Act, Art 1, 16–119, 1988 [In Farsi].
100. Napier v Scottish Ministers [2004] SLT 555.
101. *Estelle*, 429 U.S. at 103.
102. James Q. Whitman, *SYMPOSIUM: Model Penal Code: Sentencing: A Plea Against Retributivism*, 7 Buff. Crim. L. R. 85 (2003).
103. Jeremy Bentham, jurist and political reformer, is the philosopher whose name is most closely associated with the foundational era of the modern utilitarian tradition.
104. Jeremy Bentham, *Principles of Penal Law*, in The Works of Jeremy Bentham, 365, 401 (John Bowring ed. 1843).
105. James Whiteman, *supra* note 102, at 3.
106. Franklin E. Zimring & Gordon Hawkins, *Dangerousness and Criminal Justice*, 85 Mich. L. Rev. 481 (1986).
107. See Model Penal Code § 1.13(9) (1962). *Mens rea* elements concern the offender's degree of culpability, which most criminal offenses define in terms of the offender's subjective state of mind, such as intent. Id. 1.13(9) (b). Attendant circumstance elements require the existence of a specified state of affairs and do not depend on the offender's state of mind. Id. 1.13(9) (c-d).
108. Richard S. Frase, *Excessive Prison Sentences, Punishment Goals, and the Eighth Amendment: "Proportionality" Relative to What?*, 89 Minn. L. Rev. 571, 574 (2005).
109. Gregg v. Georgia, 428 U.S. 153, 183 (1976) (plurality opinion). See also Hudson v. McMillian, 503 U.S. 1, 5 (1992).

Chapter 6

Corporal Punishment and Human Rights

> Punishment that transgresses today's broad and idealistic concepts of dignity, civilized standards, humanity, and decency offends the Eighth Amendment. Therefore, the government is prohibited from imposing a penalty that is inconsistent with the dignity of man.[1]

PROHIBITION OF JUDICIAL CORPORAL PUNISHMENT UNDER INTERNATIONAL LAW

Inhuman Per Se

At first glance, judicial corporal punishment is barbaric per se, although some scholars believe that corporal punishment is not per se "cruel and unusual" under either original or modern understandings, but legislative, judicial history, and pain infliction of corporal punishment are important factors that are against this hypothesis.

For instance, mutilating punishments are barbaric because they violate the body's integrity which is a value we deeply respect in our civilization, and because they seem like a throwback to our cannibalistic past.

The main challenge to the proposed systems of judicial corporal punishment constitutes cruel and unusual punishment. However, the predecessors clearly accepted corporal punishment as a viable alternative to other forms of criminal punishment. The prison system did not truly begin to develop in that era. Before that, towns had stocks, pillories, and whipping posts to deal with criminals.

A survey of mild punishment provides further Enlightenment perspective on cruel and unusual punishment. "Cruel" is defined as brutal, savage, or barbarous. "Unusual" means scarce, peculiar, or abnormal. "Cruel and unusual punishment" means unnecessary and wanton infliction of pain. "Wanton" means unconscionable, unbridled, or unrestrained. "Unnecessary" is defined as needless or gratuitous.[2]

We will now consider judicial corporal punishment as a savage and barbarous practice. But it is still a question whether whipping was intended by the predecessors to be excluded per se as a form of punishment. It appears, however, that the predecessors did not consider whipping to be cruel and unusual. This view is evidenced by several facts. First, the evidence from the history debates indicates acceptance of corporal punishment. Second, corporal punishment was not a severe form of punishment in ancient era. Third, the early laws of the nations provided for the corporal punishment of offenders.

Wiedeman[3] believed the cruel and unusual punishment standard to be flexible and open to wider interpretation than other constitutional provisions. It is important to note that at no time has corporal punishment been ruled unconstitutional. Second, if the state can impose corporal punishment on children, through teachers, without a hearing, surely the state can impose a substantially similar penalty on criminals after they have been duly convicted in a court of law. Wiedeman preferred the method of administering the punishment would be by flogging for violent, noncapital crimes and for the more serious property crimes. Less physically painful punishment such as the pillory could be used for less serious crimes and the majority of "victimless" crimes.[4]

As mentioned earlier, flogging is punishment for certain types of consensual homosexual acts and other crimes. This is common in Iranian criminal justice systems and other Islamic criminal justice systems.[5] The main issue is whether imposing corporal punishments, such as flogging by conditions and procedures that have been prescribed by Islamic criminal justice systems, is inherently cruel and unusual. Flogging is an inhumane and barbarous type of punishment.

Proportionality Analysis

Provisions against cruel and unusual punishment are aimed primarily at the kind of punishment imposed, not its degree. Nevertheless, where the degree of a sentence imposed on one convicted of crime is so disproportionate to the offense committed as to shock the moral sense of the community, the punishment is prohibited. In determining whether the degree offends a prohibition against cruel and unusual punishment, the courts will look to such matters as the nature of the offense, the character of the offender, the penalties imposed in the jurisdiction for other offenses, and the penalties imposed in other jurisdictions for the same offense.

The Proportionality Doctrine states, in part, that the "Cruel and Unusual Punishment Clause" requires some measure of proportionality in criminal cases between the punishment imposed and the offense committed. This proportionality principle is not symmetrical. That is, Proportionality Doctrine forbids only those punishments that are disproportionately severe, not those that are disproportionately lenient.

There are three objective criteria from prior cases for resolving claims of disproportionality: (1) "the gravity of the offense compared to the severity of the penalty," (2) "the sentence imposed for commission of the same crime in other jurisdictions," and (3) "the sentence imposed upon other criminals in the same jurisdiction."[6]

Under Iran's law, the infliction of punishment should be just and commensurate with the crime committed. Here justice is done only when the offender is appropriately punished without excess. It is an important aspect of Islamic law of crimes that whatever punishment is to be meted out or inflicted on the offender for committing the crime should be proportionate to the harm inflicted by him without any excess.[7] For example, in the case of false accusation of unlawful intercourse (*qadhf*), anyone who commits it, according to the Holy Quran, is punished with eighty lashes.[8] It means if eighty lashes are awarded for this offense, the punishment is commensurate or proportionate to the harm inflicted. But if the punishment awarded is 100 lashes or tongue removal, then it is not proportionate to the harm inflicted. When punishment is inflicted in excess according to Quranic verses, this means transgressing beyond the limits set by God.[9]

Wisdom behind the amputation of the hand under Islamic law for the theft of property worth 1.4 Dinar or above is intended to provide an effective means of protecting people's property. The underlying reasoning supports the proposition that the graver the punishment the more effective it is. The question remains whether amputating a hand for a property worth 1.4 Dinar can be held to compare with 500 Dinar for loss of a hand as retribution. It is not comparable to say one should lose his hand for stealing a property worth 1.4 Dinar as equivalent to 500 Dinars as a retribution for the loss of a hand so damaged. If there is anything that the comparison tends to show, it is that they both provide protection to property and human life. In short, the 1.4 Dinar for cutting the hand and 500 Dinars as the *qisas* for the loss of a hand are made completely for different purposes.

For example, the thief who steals food is not subject to amputation. Perhaps this could be extended to the thief who, while not literally starving, lives in poverty in a society where the majority of the wealth is concentrated in the hands of a privileged minority. Accounts could also be taken of a psychological disorder, such as compulsive theft or lying, before deciding that *hudud* penalties were called for. The option of *taazir* punishments and civil remedies is not foreclosed. The mentally disabled are exempt from responsibility for violating these laws. Since medical research shows alcoholism is a disease, punishment for the crime of drinking should be suspended and conditioned on the convict seeking treatment for his illness. Likewise, children are not to receive the *hudud* penalties. Some Islamic law schools rule that puberty begins as young as age nine. Modern psychology, however, demonstrates that puberty itself is not the onset of adulthood, but an intermediate phase in human development. Therefore, it is plausible to decide that these penalties are only applicable to adults, just inapplicable to children. This could spare teenagers who violate the law from the most severe penalties.[10]

The US Supreme Court explained that the Founders understood the "Cruel and Unusual Punishment Clause" primarily as a protection against barbarous punishments such as whippings and ear removal. The punishment clause was intended to encompass new situations and contexts that the Framers could not have foreseen. "A principle, to be vital, must be capable of wider application than the mischief which gave it birth." As part of its analysis, the court compared the punishment of cadena temporal with punishments for other crimes in the same jurisdiction and with the punishments for forgery in other jurisdictions.[11] This process of comparing sentences has become an integral part of current Supreme Court proportionality analysis.

The US Supreme Court has not had occasion to apply these principles to statutorily authorized and judicially imposed whippings of criminal offenders as punishment for criminal conduct.

Reviewing a case in Iran: Mohsen Mofidi had been convicted of charges including possession of a medicine containing alcohol, consuming alcohol in the early 1980s, possession of a television satellite dish, and aiding and abetting his sister's corruption in having boyfriends. He was sentenced to eighty lashes, to be carried out on completion of a four-month prison sentence. On February 11th, the twenty-fifth anniversary of the revolution in Iran, the remainder of his prison sentence was suspended, and the flogging was scheduled to take place on the day of his release. It is reported that Mofidi was kept in extremely poor conditions at Qasr prison.

Judicial corporal punishments in Iran are cruel and unusual per se and unlawful because they entail key elements of torture or ill-treatment, including the deliberate infliction of severe pain and suffering as a punishment. The UN Human Rights Committee has stated that the prohibition of torture and ill-treatment under the International Covenant on Civil and Political Rights "must extend to corporal punishment."[12] Amnesty International opposes the punishment of flogging and has long called on the Iranian authorities to cease this practice.[13] Amnesty International continues to urge the government to conduct an immediate investigation into the death of Mohsen Mofidi and to make the findings public.

Contemporary Standards of Society

The evolving standards of decency that mark the progress of a maturing society are the final resort for applying the cruel and unusual punishment definition on corporal punishment statutes. An important reason why bodily punishment is thought of with repugnance is that they have been historically linked to the process of torture.

In many cases, the two terms are synonymous, often what one individual would call a just form of punishment another would term torture. In many cases, the actual punishment which society imposed was preceded by torture.

Although some scholars believe corporal punishment may appear to be a barbaric solution to the problems of a civilized society, others believe it is in fact a reasonable, rational alternative to the systemic prison overcrowding and rampant recidivism that are part of our current approach to crime and criminals.

The Supreme Court has held that the Eighth Amendment not only precludes the government from inflicting punishments believed by the Framers to be cruel and unusual, but it also precludes punishments that are inconsistent with contemporary values. The Eighth Amendment is not bound by the sparing humanitarian concessions of our forebears. Hence, the court has taken a dual-interpretative position. In one sense, the court has adopted an originalist point of view by holding that punishments intended by the Framers to be forbidden continue to be forbidden today. This appears to be true even if a punishment thought to be barbaric in 1791 were to become popular today. In a second sense, the court has taken a progressive view in examining the Eighth Amendment considering contemporary values and penological evidence. "Punishment that transgresses today's broad and idealistic concepts of dignity, civilized standards, humanity, and decency offends the Eighth Amendment. Therefore, the government is prohibited from imposing a penalty that is inconsistent with the dignity of man."[14]

How does a reviewing court determine society's contemporary values? The court defers to the decisions of the people's representatives. The *State v. Cannon*[15] court stated the following:

> What better way is there for the people to express an enlightened attitude toward the punishment of crime than through their elected representatives, the members of the General Assembly who, indeed, hold their office for the very purpose of expressing the will and beliefs of the people who elected them.

The court reasoned that the Delaware Legislature deserved deference in this context because it had historically responded to public opinion concerning punishments, as evinced by its abolition of the use of the pillory, drawing and quartering, death by burning, and other forms of punishment. The court, noting that Great Britain did not abolish whipping until 1948 and that Canada maintained whipping as a punishment until 1957, stated,

> It does not seem to us that a punishment so recently in use in the country that leads the world in the administration of justice may be held to be a barbarity that, as a matter of constitutional law, must be deemed cruel and unusual.[16]

The court also believed it was important that in no state had whipping been abolished by judicial decree; rather, it had been a legislative decision in every instance. Accordingly, the court held that whipping did not violate the state Constitution or the Eighth Amendment. The court remanded the case to the trial court with instructions to conduct a hearing as to whether the defendant was mentally fit to receive the lashes. On remand, the trial judge remitted the whipping portion of the sentence without a hearing.[17]

The debate over the application of the cruel and unusual punishment to the practice of corporal punishment includes ways that the words "cruel," "unusual," and "punishment" have changed their meanings. The debate surrounds whether the application of the Cruel and Unusual Punishments should be tied to perceptions of values and customs contemporaneous with its enactment, or whether the principle must ever reflect current, evolving, presumably progressive, values.

Delaware court invited the state legislature to abolish the punishment of whipping as inconsistent with contemporary mores (something the legislature did in 1973). And even in the harsh climate of the late 1980s, a firm believer as Justice Scalia[18] admitted that flogging had become too uncomfortable a practice not to be banned. Nevertheless, it is remarkable how difficult American lawyers have found it to uncover some clear argument against the practice of flogging, even at the height of the era of prison reform.[19] How whipping as a formal punishment that is not deeply rooted in Iran's culture, and background can be applied.

Similarly, in Iran amputation for theft and brigandage (*moharebeh*) are not punishments in every civilized society. In fact, for the state to tolerate them would run afoul of human rights norms which declare that no one should be deprived of his property without due process of law.

Thus, because personal dignity and humanity are highly valued in current societies, then punishments that violate these values would have to be deemed problematic and in contrast to the idealism embodied in the ban on cruel and unusual punishment.

PROHIBITION OF JUDICIAL CORPORAL PUNISHMENTS IN THE UNITED STATES AND ISLAMIC CRIMINAL JUSTICE SYSTEMS

Legislative Story

In the United States, the Northwest Territory adopted an act which provided that people convicted of arson, robbery, burglary, or obstructing authority could be publicly whipped in addition to other forms of punishment in 1788.[20] An act in 1795 made larceny punishable by a lashing, and an act in 1805 punished horse thieves with as many as two hundred stripes as well as other penalties.[21]

In contrast to these penalties, other crimes were punishable with fewer lashes. For example, a Boston court sentenced a burglar to be hanged, five thieves to be whipped, two greater thieves to be set on the gallows, and one counterfeiter set on the pillory. Later, the same Boston court ordered eleven offenders to be whipped. Another offender, appointed to execute the whipping, persisted in being tender of strokes, contrary to the orders of the official supervising the punishment. Eventually, the official seized the whip, turned it on the whipper, and then completed the task personally. According to one account, "the citizens who were assembled complimented the Sheriff with three cheers for the manly determined manner in which he executed his duty."[22]

In 1790, Congress enacted the nation's first criminal law that provided for public whipping of thieves.[23] There were other federal statutes that provided for whipping as a form of punishment. For example, certain postal crimes were punished with up to forty lashes under a statute enacted in 1799,[24] and in 1801 a federal statute was enacted delegating to justices of the peace in Washington, DC, the authority to punish offenders with whipping, imprisonment, and a fine of 500 pounds of tobacco.[25] Whipping and standing in the stock continued to be punishments under federal law until 1839.[26] In 1898, the Virginia Legislature provided for the whipping of male youths.[27]

Although whipping was abolished for federal offenders in 1839, whipping continued in several states well into the twentieth century. For example, the final whipping in Maryland took place in 1948. Whipping was not statutorily abolished in Maryland until 1953.[28] Similarly, the last statutorily authorized whipping as punishment for a crime in Delaware was on June 16, 1952.[29] The crime was breaking and entering, for which the defendant received twenty lashes.[30] Although not administered after 1952, whipping was provided for by statute in Delaware until 1986. In fact, defendants in two separate cases during the 1960s were sentenced to be whipped. For reasons discussed below, however, neither sentence was executed. A total of 1,607 individuals were subjected to whipping in Delaware between 1900 and 1942.[31] State legislatures enacted chemical castration laws and recently, by way of the caning of Michael Fay in Singapore, have expressed renewed interest in corporal punishment.

Judicial Story

Some early state courts specifically declared whipping constitutionality permissible. Despite the court decisions, whipping as a mode of punishment has historically been subject to constant attack. During the nineteenth century, it fell into general disuse. Many scholars and jurists opposed its utilization altogether. Others while not entirely opposing it, favored strict limitations on its use. In 1820, for example, Justice Taylor[32] writing an opinion for the North Carolina Supreme Court asserted: "Public corporal punishment for any offense impresses an indelible stigma on the character and ought to be inflicted on those offenses only which are infamous in their nature." In 1851, Justice Lipscomb of the Texas Supreme Court went so far as to assert: "Among all nations of civilized man, from the earliest ages, the infliction of strips has been considered more degrading than death itself."

The fact is courts routinely sentenced offenders to be lashed, which is another reason for believing that the Framers of the US Constitution did not consider corporal punishment to be cruel and unusual punishment. One can surmise that the judges must have believed that whipping punishment was consistent with their new Constitution. In addition to the other evidence of judicially imposed whippings discussed above, there are several reported decisions from which the constitutionality of whipping can be inferred. For example, the Illinois Supreme Court stated in 1930 that "the law is well settled that the record shall affirmatively show the defendant was present in court when sentence was imposed, if there is any corporal punishment administered."[33] Courts often assumed that corporal punishment was constitutional if the defendant's other rights were not violated. Where the issue was not addressed by the courts, the reason for the assumption was presumably because the parties did not raise the issue or that whipping was so commonly accepted that a defendant would not have raised the cruel and unusual defense.[34]

In support of the assertion that corporal punishment was not considered cruel and unusual punishment is that several courts directly addressed the issue and concluded that whippings were not repugnant to the Constitution. In *Foote v. State,*[35] a defendant, sentenced to sixty days in jail and seven stripes for beating his wife, challenged the imposition of whipping as violative of the Eighth Amendment and its counterpart provision in the Maryland Constitution. Although the Maryland Court concluded that the Eighth Amendment was not applicable to the state, it analyzed the case under the cruel and unusual punishment clause of the Maryland Constitution. The court held:

> The terms cruel and unusual pains and penalties, and cruel or unusual punishment, have been incorporated in each successive Constitution in this State from 1776 to the present time. That the punishment of whipping was not considered a cruel or unusual punishment, and, therefore, coming within the prohibition of the Constitution, is most conclusively shown by the fact that the punishment by whipping was recognized by the statute law of the State under all these Constitutions, certainly down to the Constitution of 1864.[36]

When, therefore, we find that the people who made this Constitution, and who must be presumed to understand the meaning of the terms they use, have from the time these words were first incorporated in 1776 down to 1882, a period of more than a hundred years, through several successive legislatures, uniformly held that the punishment of whipping was not included in that class which the Constitution forbids, we should violate the plainest principles of the construction of statutes now to decide otherwise. We have not only the contemporaneous but also the continued exposition of the meaning of the words in this long course of legislative construction, upheld and continually enforced by the courts, in the imposition of the punishment.

If authority be wanted for the position we have taken, that whipping is not the cruel or unusual punishment forbidden by the Bill of Rights, it may be found in the decisions of some of the states as well as of the Federal Courts. Thus, the Maryland Court of Appeals held that whipping did not violate the cruel and unusual punishment clause of the Maryland Constitution.

In 1824, the Virginia Supreme Court, in *Aldridge v. Commonwealth,*[37] relied on the principle of separation of powers to uphold Virginia's legislation providing for whipping of offenders. Four years later, in *Commonwealth v. Wyatt,*[38] the Virginia Supreme Court held that whipping was "odious but cannot be said to be *unusual.*"

Several other cases have gone to the highest court of a state on this issue. For example, the Supreme Court of the Territory of New Mexico addressed the issue in *Garcia v. Territory of New Mexico,*[39] where the court sentenced a mule thief to thirty stripes, as provided for by statute. The court stated the following:

> All punishment is more or less cruel, and the kind of punishment to be inflicted upon criminals to induce reformation and repress and deter the thief from a repetition of his larcenies has generally been left to the sound discretion of the law-making power.

The word cruel, as used in the amendatory article of the Constitution, was no doubt intended to prohibit a resort to the process of torture, resorted to so many centuries as a means of extorting confessions from suspected criminals, under the sanction of the civil law. It was never designed to abridge or limit the selection by the law-making power of such kind of punishment and suppression of crime. If a father, without the charge of cruelty, may administer stripes to his vicious and disobedient child, may not the supreme power of a territory, state, or nation administer the same kind of punishment to its vicious and lawless citizens? However averse the court may be to this mode of punishment, it cannot authorize the court in disregarding and annulling the law providing for the punishment of this crime, and, until repealed, it is the duty of the court to enforce it.

In addition, the Tennessee Supreme Court, in *Cornell v. State,*[40] held in 1881 that corporal punishment could be imposed, but only if sanctioned either by the legislature or a law or regulation made for the government of the convicts by the county court in due form, at a regular session, or the governing authorities of the corporate town by whom the workhouse has been established. The Arkansas Supreme Court reached a similar conclusion in 1884.[41] In contrast to these decisions, at least two courts stated, in dicta, that the use of the whipping post was cruel. Nevertheless, the weight of the evidence supports the conclusion that the Framers did not consider whipping to be a cruel and unusual mode of punishment.

The most significant state court decisions originated in Delaware. In 1963, the Supreme Court of Delaware issued two opinions directly addressing whether a state may statutorily permit or mandate whipping as a form of punishment.[42] In 1961, Franklin Cannon pled guilty to grand larceny. He was sentenced to three years of imprisonment and a whipping of twenty lashes. The sentence was suspended to probation, but it was reinstated after the defendant violated the terms of his probation. He appealed the sentence to the Supreme Court of Delaware. Mr. Cannon challenged the whipping portion of his sentence as violative of the Delaware Constitution and the Eighth Amendment.

The parties and the court agreed that whipping was not considered cruel and unusual at the time of the adoption of the Constitution. Within the context of analyzing the prohibition, under the Delaware Constitution, of cruel punishments, the court concluded that the Framers of the Delaware Constitution intended to abolish punishments prohibited in England by the so-called Bill of Rights of England.[43] These were the cruel and barbarous punishments on occasion formerly imposed in England by the Crown. They were punishments considered at the time to be unnecessarily cruel and bordering upon outright torture such as breaking on the wheel, public dissection, and the like.

The court concluded that whipping was not per se violative of the Delaware Constitution at the time of its ratification. Implicit in the court's decision was the extension of this reasoning to the Eighth Amendment. This extension, however, did not conclude the court's inquiry.[44]

Later that same year, the Delaware Supreme Court reaffirmed the rationale of *State v. Cannon*[45] in *Balser v. State.*[46] In *Balser,* a defendant convicted of robbery challenged his sentence to twenty lashes as being constitutionally repugnant upon the same theories as were asserted by the defendant in *State v. Cannon.* The court summarily disposed of the issue, referring to its decision in *State v. Cannon.* Again, however, the whipping did not take place. The court reversed the sentence on other grounds, ordered a resentencing, and the Governor of the State of Delaware removed the whipping portion of the sentence through a commutation of the sentence.

Corporal punishment has never been held by United States courts per se to violate the Eighth Amendment. Courts routinely sentenced offenders to be whipped in early America. Courts that have considered whether whipping is cruel and unusual punishment have concluded that it is not. Finally, this conclusion is reinforced by the fact that whipping continued well beyond the lives of the Framers of the Constitution.[47] The conclusion that whipping was not considered cruel and unusual at the time of the adoption of the Eighth Amendment does not end the constitutional inquiry.

Therefore, it will ordinarily be cumulative: If a punishment is unusually severe, if there is a strong probability that it is inflicted arbitrarily, if it is substantially rejected by contemporary society, and if there is no reason to believe that it serves any penal purpose more effectively than some less severe punishment, then the continued infliction of that punishment violates the command of the Clause that the state may not inflict inhuman and uncivilized punishments upon those convicted of crimes.

Cultural Relativism Notion to Justify Harsh Punishments

The suggestion from some Islamic states that religious law forbids abolition of the capital and corporal punishments constitutes an important obstacle to universal abolition of harsh punishments. International human rights standards, as embodied in the UN treaties, represent the opposite end of the political spectrum from conservative religious fundamentalism.

With the advent of Islamic fundamentalism in the 1970s, more and more Islamic states began objecting to international norms for human rights and abolition of the harsh punishments, as being contrary to *Sharia,*[48] the historically formulated traditional law of Islam.[49]

To justify the conflict between Theocracy and principles of human rights, we can apply the cultural relativism notion to conclude that current international human rights norms do not necessarily apply to Islamic states or by considering the evolution of Islamic law we can say, Islamic laws need to be updated and meet demands of the modern time.

Cultural relativism is used in international law to describe a "cultural chasm" in which irreconcilable cultural differences preclude the pervasive realization of substantive international law and morality. According to *Bridging the Cultural Chasm* article: "Because all cultures are equal, according to this view, the human rights practices of different cultures must be equally tolerated."[50]

The theory of cultural relativism thus supports the view that different regions, cultures, and traditions should have different norms. Based on Samuel P. Huntington's controversial *Foreign Affairs* article, it is possible to carve the world into several civilizational regions, including, in addition to the West, an "Islamic civilization" and a "Confucian civilization."[51]

By considering this theory, Islamic criminal justice systems with harsh punishments, stung by criticism of their human rights practices, can adopt cultural relativism as a rationale for not fully implementing international human rights norms.

Based on the Islamic Declaration of Human Rights: "All the rights and freedoms stipulated in this Declaration are subject to the Islamic *Sharia*."[52] Clarifying things even further is Article 25, which provides that the "*Sharia* is the only source of reference for the explanation or clarification of any of the articles of this Declaration."[53]

The question is whether classical Islamic law envisions the implementation of any specific criminal justice system as a matter of religious concern. Islamic law arose out of various sources, but more specifically from the teachings of the prophet Muhammad. It developed in a formal sense during the seventh and eighth centuries (670–720 AD). Its two most important elements are the *Sharia* and the *fiqh*. *Sharia* refers to the sacred laws and ways of life proscribed by God. The Quran and the *sunna* or *sunnah* comprises the *Sharia*. These are considered the most important sources of Islamic law. The Quran is the primary source of guidance because it is regarded as the spoken word of God,[54] and the *sunnah* refers to the words and actions of the prophet. The *Sharia* is said to deal with ideology and faith, behavior and manners, and practical daily matters. It is a comprehensive body of norms covering "every aspect of life including international, constitutional, administrative, criminal, civil, family, and religion." The *fiqh*,[55] or Islamic jurisprudence, on the other hand, refers to "the legal rulings of the Muslim scholars derived from the *sharia*."[56]

The problem is how the Islamic Declaration of Human Rights purports to interpret *Sharia* as a working legal code in a twentieth-century world leaving interpretations of the eight-hundred-year-old *Sharia* to individual states is what Surya Praka Sinha, an advocate of civilizational norms, calls "extreme relativism run amok, wherein a state becomes its own normative arbiter."[57]

In addition, there is a fatal flaw in the notion that civilizational norms based upon the primacy of communal over individual rights can even have their own standards of human rights. Groups are not human; individuals are. Without the individual, there is no group, yet the converse cannot be said. Thus, human rights are, of their very essence, a recognition that individuals are human and possessed certain rights and freedoms that the community cannot take away.[58] Thus the act of the state in using barbaric punishments is the ultimate denial of individuality; it says that the state is stronger than the individual. The source of an individual's human rights is the state rather than the individual's humanity. The state wields its power to extinguish the life and dignity of humans who, in the view of the state, cross the line and encroach upon what the state believes is necessary to hold on to that power.[59]

Islamic criminal justice systems by using flogging and body amputation deny what is arguably an emerging international law norm. It seems Islamic criminal justice systems invoke this justification as an excuse to legitimate their undemocratic regimes and human rights policies outside of international law norms. Therefore, harsh punishments are political, rather than cultural, in nature.[60]

The fact is, there can be no question that the *Sharia* was developed within a clear historical context. Like the Quran, the tradition, the second most important source of Islamic law, is also a response to specific historical circumstances. Indeed, countless traditions strive to explain the historical context in which a certain revelation was revealed.[61]

THE FUTURE OF JUDICIAL CORPORAL PUNISHMENTS IN ISLAMIC CRIMINAL JUSTICE SYSTEMS

Can Islamic Criminal Justice System Evolve?

The primary religion in each nation molds the individual country's ideology regarding the penal system and policy. Although there are some bases for the claim that capital and corporal punishments are part of Islamic law, its scope, however, is considerably truncated; these punishments are a mandatory penalty under the *Sharia* for only a small category of crimes.

Again the *Sharia* was developed within a clear historical context. Like the Quran, the tradition, the second most important source of Islamic law, is also a response to specific historical circumstances. Indeed, countless traditions strive to explain the historical context in which a certain revelation was revealed.[62]

Islam professes the basic principle that everyone has the right to life and dignity. However, this principle stated in the Quran allows for an exception. Killing and physical punishments are only allowed when a court of law demands it: "Do not kill a Soul which God has made sacred except through the due process of law." Therefore, this exception authorizes the administration of capital punishment when Islamic law dictates. Intriguingly, the Islamic law position would seem to be the same as that found in the Fifth Amendment to the US Constitution and such international instruments as the European Convention on Human Rights.[63]

Iran has ratified the International Covenant on Civil and Political Rights concerning Article 6(2). It seems Iran has accepted international norms. Therefore, in accordance with Article 6(2) of the International Covenant on Civil, the imposition of the harsh punishments for non-serious crimes is contrary to the Covenant.[64] And, crimes for which Islamic Penal Code mandates the death penalty and corporal punishments cannot by any effort at interpretation be deemed to be the "most serious crimes" for which the capital or corporal punishment may be imposed.

Reynaldo Galindo Pohl, formerly Special Rapporteur of the Commission on Human Rights on Iran, observed that

> there are groups of Islamic legal scholars and practitioners who recommend the abolition of the death penalty for political crimes on the ground that it is contrary to Islamic law. They state that the number of crimes punishable by death is limited.[65]

Islamic law has an ability to demonstrate some degree of flexibility in the interpretation of harsh punishment. Although, it appears that religion is little more than a pretext to justify a resort to harsh penalties that are driven by backward and repressive attitudes in the area of criminal law.

As we discussed, the *Sharia* specifically permits the imposition of capital and corporal punishments only for four *hudud* offenses and *qisas* committed with deliberate intent. Even then, the evidentiary requirements for the conviction of *hudud* crimes ensure that punishment will be rare, while the Quran pointedly admonishes that it is more meritorious to pardon a murderer than to seek retaliation. While it has been argued that Islamic law governs the social order of Islamic societies, this has not prevented the *Sharia's* from being amended or ignored when the environment dictated. This has been referred to as the doctrine of necessity. The doctrine of necessity dispenses Muslims from observing religious laws when the situation or environment dictates otherwise.[66]

Enforcing harsh punishments for different crimes appears more as a political slogan than a return to past realities in which the Muslim state was able to escape "the restrictions of the jurists bureaucracy to enforce its own decrees." Mandating capital or corporal punishments are in the area of *taazir* (discretionary punishment) characterized as manifestations of the will of Muslim states, not the commands of Islamic law. We should determine their application by the demands of a specific culture and time.

It is unlikely at any rate that any contemporary laws mandating capital punishment coincide with the values of classical Islamic law. For offenses and punishments that were both defined and imposed according to the discretion of the judge or ruler and for the small number of *hudud* offenses, equally orthodox scholars differed as to each *hadd's* scope and application, often in significant details. We can restrict the use of harsh punishment, as did the Quranic exhortation to pardon those who commit a *qisas* offense. Upon *ijma*[67] on the details of these offenses becomes solidified, one may argue that God's meaning has finally been understood: the *hadith*[68] promises that "My community shall never agree upon an error."[69]

If we seek to justify judicial corporal punishments in the Islamic penal codes by claiming authorization from God betrays willful disavowal of Islam's legal history. In my view, corporal punishment constitutes a perversion of the values of Islamic faith. Conservative Islamic states fighting to retain harsh punishments use religious arguments in order to force the debate into one of cultural or religious norms. The Bible also contemplates capital punishment for such crimes as magic, violation of the Sabbath, blasphemy, adultery, homosexuality, relations with animals, incest, and rape.[70] Although Judeo and Christian jurists will rarely argue that this ancient text dictates contemporary legal practice.

Islamic punishments originated in the Arab tribal system of punishment. Imam Bukhari narrated a *hadith* (tradition) on the authority of Ibn Abbas that the law of retaliation was originally prescribed to the Israelites.[71] It shows these punishments belong to many ancient cultures. If a poll were conducted tomorrow in Iran and other Islamic countries, we would find considerable support for these punishments. Why do cruel and unusual punishments that are not deeply rooted in Iran's cultural and background continue to be applied? In determining the possibility of moratorium or abolition of these punishments, we should contemplate that the application of *hudud* (prescribed punishments) to be conditional upon the society, which must be just before this punishment, can be effectively and consistently applied. Thus, Islamic laws need to be reformed to comply with the demands of modernity.

Politics and Judicial Corporal Punishment in Authoritarian Regimes

Harsh punishments are an important tool in penal policy of many authoritarian regimes. Permanent removal of political offenders or using certain types of corporal punishments to achieve temporary incapacitation is the best solution for authoritarian governments to suppress political dissidents. Hardline governments have used harsh punishments on a grand scale in political conflict to threat an opposition group.

The use of inhuman punishments by Hitler, Stalin, and Mussolini demonstrates the importance of government structure toward a harsh penal policy.[72]

Twentieth-century fascist and totalitarian regimes had obvious affection for high rates of cruel punishments. In Europe, the rapid move toward more humane punishments happened after the change of regimes and fall of the Soviet Union.[73] In the contemporary era, totalitarian regimes still continue the high rate of harsh punishments. The practice of inhumane punishments in countries such as Iran, Saudi Arabia, Libya, and Syria shows the relationship between execution rates and dictatorship. (Please see figure 6.1.)

But the question is how likely the authoritarian nations are to abolish judicial corporal punishments?

I've reviewed the prospects for change in the harsh penal policy of Islamic criminal justice systems in the following stages:

1. Political reform or change of regime
2. Reform of contemporary criminal justice systems

Iran seems a good likely candidate for liberalization in the near future. But if a country with a harsh justice system lacks hardline restrictions, it will be possible to abolish capital and corporal punishments after reform of the criminal justice system. Although Iran's citizenry is well educated, it's more tightly controlled. Therefore, Iran is less vulnerable to reform.

Finally, what are the possibilities for democratization in Islamic criminal justice systems with a harsh justice system during the next fifteen to twenty years? Despite rapid growth in the number and scale of public protests, the current countries with Islamic criminal justice systems still have a strong

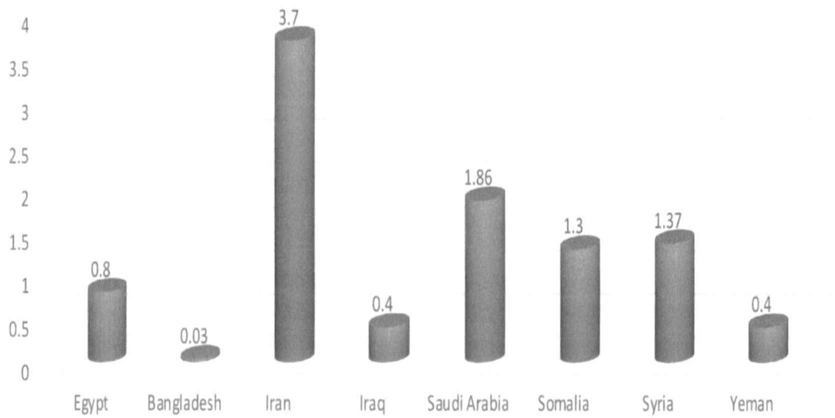

Figure 6.1 Execution Rates in Islamic Countries per Million Population. *Source*: Figure created by author.

grip on state and society. We might think democratic reforms tend to foster decline of the corporal/capital punishments and eventual abolition. But when we review the consequence of Arab Springs in the Middle East, there is no evidence that proves all political changes will be in the direction of more democratic government and increased respect for human rights.

The voluntary abolition of harsh punishments by Islamic criminal justice systems has not been a common occurrence in the Middle East. For the Islamic nations with a harsh penal policy, the financial expenses of capital or corporal punishments are small, and super due process for capital or corporal cases is not provided in the Islamic criminal justice systems. Several changes in procedural reforms and appeal process of these cases will increase the system costs, but such changes have yet to start in those countries.

The rate of harsh punishments in authoritarian Middle Eastern countries is increasing and probably will continue to increase. Some of these increases are a function of political changes, and there is less international attention to executions or public corporal punishments in Islamic criminal justice systems.

The study on Iran shows that there is a relationship between the use of harsh punishments (death penalty or corporal punishment) and political events. Iran's execution rate jumped drastically since the 1979 Islamic Revolution, and the use of inhumane judicial corporal punishment was the invention of the Islamic Revolution and the Islamization of laws. The first year after the revolution bore witness to the execution of a number of politicians, generals, high rank officials, and secret police agents of the former regime. The execution rate had a sharp increase in 1981 following the bloody suppression of the opposition groups. Amnesty International recorded more than 2,616 executions in 1981. Although there was a fall in the number of executions in subsequent years until 1988, in summer of 1988, a large number of political prisoners were executed.

> Iranian authorities flogged four political prisoners in prisons across the country in 2019, according to a report from *Iran News Wire*. On June 8, 2019, authorities flogged Azeri rights activists Ali Azizi and Eliar Hosseinzadeh for "disturbing public order," by taking part in the November 2019 protests in the city of Orumiyeh. Prison officials at Greater Tehran Penitentiary flogged protester Mohamad Bagher Souri on the same day. Authorities flogged Tehran bus driver and labor activist Rasoul Taleb Moghadam seventy-four times for taking part in a peaceful Labor Day gathering outside parliament in 2019.

In recent years, we can still see the relationship between political events and the use of cruel punishments in Iran. The number of executions in Iran dropped significantly with the highest number of executions in July 2009, when the Green Movement and post-election protests started. In the aftermath of the 12 June presidential election, Mahmoud Ahmadinejad was declared the winner. Thus millions of people started protests, thousands were arrested, and a number of people were executed. From 12 June to the Presidential Inauguration Day on 5 August, about 115 executions were recorded. Most of these were prosecuted with the charge of *moharebeh*[74] for having taken part in protests against fraud in elections.

The majority of executions and other forms of harsh punishments in authoritarian regimes take place in Iran and Saudi Arabia[75] (please see table 6.1). Both nations remain a retentionist state with one of the highest records of executions in the world, especially in relation to its population. Middle Eastern countries with Islamic criminal justice systems that practise *Sharia* law as the source of their criminal justice system are associated with the use of capital and corporal punishments as retribution for the largest variety of crimes.

The laws of the Islamic retentionist countries punish by death or corporal punishment a very large number of offenses, including offenses that are not considered among the most serious crimes. For example, the. revised Penal Code in Iran has been extended to apostasy and widened its scope in the case of vaguely worded offenses, such as corruption on earth.

Although all Islamic retentionist nations are a party to the ICCPR and the CRC, the provisions of those international human rights instruments relevant to the death penalty and prohibition of other types of cruel and unusual punishments are widely disregarded. The recommendations addressed to the government of the Islamic Republic of Iran by the treaty bodies in charge of the examination of the respect for these conventions have been left unimplemented for years, in particular with regard to gender-neutral age of majority, end to sentencing and execution of juvenile offenders, restriction of the scope of the death penalty, and end to public executions and judicial corporal punishments.

Table 6.1 Number of Executions by Islamic States since 2019

Country	Total	2019	2020	2021
Iran	811	251	246	314
Saudi Arabia	276	184	27	65
Egypt	222	32	107	83
Iraq	162	100	45	17
Somalia	44	12	11	21
Yemen	26	7	5	14
Syria	24	+	+	24
Pakistan	14	14	0	0

Source: Amnesty International Death Penalty Reports of 2019-2020 and 2021. +Amnesty International is confident that there was more than one execution.

NOTES

1. Estelle v. Gamble, 429 U.S. 97, 102 (1976).
2. Oxford Unabridged Dictionary.
3. Wiedeman, *Special Issue: Juvenile Justice and the Criminal Law: Comment: Don't Spare the Rod: A Proposed Return to Public, Corporal Punishment on Convicts.*
4. *Id.*
5. Punishment for any homosexual activity without intercourse is one hundred lashes; punishment for lesbianism is one hundred lashes.
6. Stephen Parr, *A New Perspective on the Cruel and Unusual Punishment Clause,* 68 Tenn. L. Rev. 41 (2000).
7. Mohammadreza Zafari, *Origins of Criminal Justice in Islamic Law* (Tehran, Iran: Amirkabir Publication, 1997) [In Farsi].
8. Holy Quran, Soreh Noor, 4 verse.
9. Yunesa Bambale, *Crimes and Punishments under Islamic Law*, 8 (Malthouse Press Limited, 2003).
10. Edna Lewicki, *Need Word's Collide: The Hudad Crimes of Islamic Law and International Human Rights*, 13 NYILR 43 (2000).
11. Drew Page, *Cruel and Unusual Punishment and Sodomy Statutes: The Breakdown of the Soldem v. Helm*, 56 U. Chi. L. Rev. 367 (1989).
12. See www.ohchr.org/english/bodies/hrc.
13. See www.amnesty.org.
14. Stephen Parr, *supra note* 6.
15. State v. Cannon, 190 A.2d 514, 514–515 (Del. 1963).
16. *Id.*
17. *Id.*
18. Antonin Gregory Scalia was an American jurist who served as an associate justice of the Supreme Court of the United States from 1986 until his death in 2016. He was an intellectual anchor for the originalist and textualist position in the US Supreme Court's conservative wing.
19. Whiteman, *supra* note 3.
20. See www.corpun.com.
21. *Id.*
22. Kenneth Shuster, *Halacha as a Model for American Penal Practice: A Comparison of Halachic and American Punishment Methods*, 19 Nova L. Rev. 965(1995).
23. Act of Apr. 30, 1790, ch. 9, § § 15, 16, 1 Stat. 112, 115–116 (repealed 1839). Convicted persons could be punished with as many as thirty-nine stripes under this statute.
24. Act of Mar. 2, 1799, ch. 43, § 15, 1 Stat. 733, 736 (repealed 1810).
25. United States v. More, *7 U.S. (3 Cranch) 159, 167 (1805).*
26. The Act of February 28, 1839, abolished whipping and standing in the stocks. Act of Feb. 28, 1839, ch. 36, § 5, 25 Stat. 321, 322 (1839).
27. Simeon. Baldwin, *The Restoration of Whipping as a Punishment for Crime,* 13 GREEN BAG 65, 66 (1901).

28. Daniel Hall, *When Canning Meets the Eighth Amendment: Whipping Offenders in the United States*, 4 Widenr J. Pub. L. 403 (1995).

29. DEL. CODE ANN. tit. 29, § *901* (1983) was amended to abolish flogging as a punishment by 65 Del. Laws 425 (1986). The effective date of the amendment was July 3, 1986. The crime to which the whipping penalty attached was altering, defacing, or otherwise destroying a bill or act of the General Assembly. Whipping was abolished for most other crimes in 1973. Act of Apr. 1, 1973, ch. 497, 58 Del. Laws 2.

30. Although no whippings were executed after 1952, it appears that a few judges continued to view corporal punishment as part of the state's sentencing scheme. For example, in *Balser v. State,* the defendant was sentenced to twenty lashes for a robbery conviction, Balser *v. State, 195 A.2d 757 (Del. 1963).* In *Cannon v. State,* a defendant was sentenced to three years of imprisonment and twenty lashes for the crime of larceny. *Cannon v. State, 196 A.2d 399 (Del. 1963);* For reasons discussed in this article, neither offender was flogged. In *Osburn v. State,* the trial judge commented, during the sentencing of an armed robber, that he would not sentence the defendant to be whipped because of the defendant's youth, indicating that the trial judge believed lashing adult offenders convicted of armed robbery was acceptable. *Osburn v. State, 224 A.2d 52 (Del. 1966).*

31. Daniel Hall, *supra* note 28.

32. John Louis Taylor (March 1, 1769–January 29, 1829) was an American jurist and first chief justice of the North Carolina Supreme Court.

33. People v. Moran, 174 N.E. 532, 533 (Ill. 1930); see also Ritchey v. People, 43 P. 1026, 1027 (Colo. 1896) (asserting the rule that there will be no bail in cases of corporal punishment); People v. Russell, 91 N.E. 1075 (Ill. 1910) (recognizing that the whipping of thieves is provided for by statute).

34. Kie v. United States, 27 F. 351, 358 (C.C.D. Or. 1886) (observing that the imposition of corporal punishment was constitutional if the defendant was present during the trial and sentencing proceedings); Ely v. Thompson, 10 Ky. (3 A.K. Marsh) 70, 74 (1820) (holding the imposition of corporal punishment unconstitutional where a statute deprived a defendant of due process of law); Ex parte Deane, 7 F. Cas. 306, 307 (No. 3712 C.C.D.C. 1816) (assuming the constitutionality of a Virginia law that imposed corporal punishment by allowing a town to provide a choice between corporal punishment and the imposition of a fine).

35. 59 Md. 264, 1883 WL 4110, Md., January 26, 1883.

36. *Id.*

37. 2 Va.Cas. 447, 4 Va. 447, 1824 WL 1072, Va.Gen.Ct, June Term 1824.

38. 6 Rand. 694, 27 Va. 694, 1828 WL 860, Va.Gen.Ct, November Term 1828.

39. 1 N.M. 415, 1 Gild. 415, 1869 WL 2421, N.M.Terr., January Term 1869.

40. 74 Tenn. 624, 1881 WL 4276, 6 Lea 624, Tenn., April Term 1881.

41. Werner v. State, 44 Ark. 122, 131 (1884). In *Werner,* the court held: Corporal punishment by the lash can be inflicted lawfully upon the convicts in the penitentiary for refusal to work, only under a rule or regulation made for that purpose by the board of commissioners; for all questions of discipline are deferred to their discretion by

the legislature, and it follows that the manner of punishment to be inflicted by way of correction must be prescribed by them.

42. Balser v. State, 195 A.2d 757 (Del. 1963); State v. Cannon, 190 A.2d 514 (Del. 1963).

43. *Id.*

44. *Id.*

45. State v. Cannon, 190 A.2d 514 (Del. 1963).

46. 7 Storey 206, 57 Del. 206, 195 A.2d 757, Del.Supr, November 27, 1963.

47. Daniel Hall, *supra* note 28.

48. *Sharia* was developed in the centuries following Prophet Mohammed's death in 632, and its formulation was essentially complete by the thirteenth century.

49. Joan Fitzpatrick & Alice Miller, *International Standards on the Death Penalty: Shifting Discourse*, 19 BROOK. J. INT'L L. 273, 278 (1993).

50. Christopher C. Joyner & John C. Dettling, *Bridging the Cultural Chasm: Cultural Relativism and the Future of International Law*, 20 CAL. W. INT'L L.J. 275, 275 (1990).

51. Samuel P. Huntington, *The Clash of Civilizations?* 22–25, FOREIGN AFF., Summer (1993).

52. Cairo Declaration, Art. XXIV, U.N. GAOR, *World Conf. on Human Rights*, 4th Sess., Agenda Item 5, at 10, U.N. Doc. A/CONF.157/PC/62/Add.18 (1993).

53. *Id, Art.* XXV.

54. J.N.D. Anderson, *Law as a Social Force in Islamic Culture and History*, 20 BULLETIN OF SOAS 13–40 (1957).

55. The Fiqh is a second important source of guidance for Islamic law.

56. J.N.D. Anderson, *supra* note 54.

57. Surya Prakash Sinah, *Legal Polycentricity and International Law,* 146–147 (California academic Press, 1996).

58. William A. Schabas, *Symposium: Religion's Role in the Administration of the Death Penalty Islam and the Death Penalty,* 9 Wm. & Mary Bill Rts. J. 223.

59. James H. Wyman, *Vengeance is Whose?: The Death Penalty and Cultural Relativism in International Law*, Journal of Transnational Law and Policy Summer (1997).

60. *Id.*

61. *Id.*

62. *Id.*

63. William A. Schabas, *supra note* 58, p 147.

64. U.N. Doc. CCPR/C/79/Add.25, <section> 8.

65. Report on the Human Rights Situation in the Islamic Republic of Iran by the Special Representative of the Comm'n on Human Rights, Mr. Reynoldo Galindo Pohl, pursuant to Commission Resolution 1988/69, U.N. ESCOR, Hum. Rts.Comm'n, 45th Sess., 26th mtg. <section>36, at 12, U.N. Doc. E/CN.4/1989/26 (1989).

66. Joseph Schacht, *Problems of Modern Islamic Legislation*, 12 Studia Islamica 99, 101 (1960).

67. Consensus of Opinions among Muslim Jurists.

68. Saying: Tradition of the prophet or the Imams.

69. Mohammed Hashim Kamali, *Principles of Islamic Jurisprudence*, 179 (Paul & Co Pub Consortium, 1989).

70. Exodus 21:14, 22:18; Leviticus 20:15, 24:13; Deuteronomy 21:21, 22:11, 22:25, 29:13; Numbers 13:5, 17:7, 19:19, 22:23, 33:14, 33:37.

71. Mohammad Ibn Esmaeil Bukhari; *Sahih Bokhari, vol.* 6, Hadith No. 25, 22–23 (Lebanon: Dar ‘Fekr Publication, 1401 Lunar Hejiri) [In Arabic].

72. David Johnson, *The Next Frontier*, 295 (New York: Oxford University Press, 2009), 29.

73. *Id.*

74. *Moharebeh or Resorting to arms to frighten people* is defined as an act of robbery by a group of armed men within the territory of the Islamic state that creates anarchy under which the property, privacy, safety, dignity, and religious values of the people would be violated. The crime is regarded as a war against God and his messenger.

75. Saudi Arabia follows a strict interpretation of Islamic law that prescribes the death sentence for murder, apostasy, rape, drug trafficking, highway robbery, sabotage and armed robbery.

Conclusion

Tracing the historical development of judicial corporal punishment has proven a long, involved, and at times complex process. The reinstatement of judicial corporal punishment as an alternative to imprisonment becomes more and more important with the flaws of the prison system in the twenty-first century. The United States in the last several decades has reached historically high prison population numbers—both in terms of absolute numbers and per capita rates.

If you were given a choice between fifty lashes and five years in prison, which would you choose?[1] Today some methods of corporal punishment exist in statutes in Iran and the United States. Although the US Supreme Court has officially upheld corporal punishment, many states have outlawed it by statute. But the question about cruelty is ambiguous. In the twenty-first century, there are partial voices in Islamic criminal justice systems and the United States. Compared with prison, it is difficult to see how corporal punishment is cruel. We must distinguish carefully among corporal punishments. All corporal punishments are certainly not the same. Biased voices believe that if corporal punishment can be shown not to cause any lasting damage to the body, except that it hurts then, how can we conclude that this punishment is cruel? Despite its barbarous nature, corporal punishment proponents at least want to limit its imposition in the following ways:

—Acute corporal punishment should be introduced to fill the gap between the severe punishment of prison and the non-punishment of probation.
—For the majority of property crimes, the preferred corporal punishment is that of electric shock because it can be scientifically controlled and calibrated. Shock is less violent in its application when compared with other corporal punishment such as whipping.

—For violent crimes in which the victim was terrified and humiliated and for which a local community does not wish to incarcerate, a violent corporal punishment should be considered, such as whipping. In these cases, the humiliation on the offender is seen as justifiably deserved.

Flogging as a punishment method is not in practice in the United States. However Islamic criminal justice systems of Saudi Arabia and Iran routinely use these punishments. This profound clash of attitudes was not the result of some difference in the degree of civilization. It was the result of differences in traditions of status.

A major difficulty is how to distinguish between an appropriate form of judicial corporal punishment in the United States and Islamic criminal justice systems. The most dramatic differences are related to the proportionality doctrine. Penal proportionality based on religious proportionality in Islamic criminal justice systems is completely different from the secular proportionality in the United States. For example, criminalizing fornication between a non-Muslim man and Muslim woman would not pass secular proportionality doctrine. In the United States, criminalizing sexual conduct is related to harm caused for the society rather than to the virtue of Muslims.

Punishment is a universal feature of contemporary societies. It would be a mistake to view harsh punishments as a uniform response to particular types of misconduct. In fact, how crimes are defined and their legal treatment reflect the prevailing social, cultural, political, economic, and historical conditions of a society at any given point in time. In some contexts, punishment may be normatively acceptable in certain cultures. Even within the same country over time, the legal acceptance of particular punishments changes. For instance, witchcraft in the United States was punishable by whipping in the past or flogging for fornication after the Islamic Revolution in Iran.

Foucault argued that punishment is an expression of power. He believes the shift from harsh punishments to more humane punishments, which occurred during the nineteenth century in democratic nations, suggests that authoritarian countries have for some reason not fully undergone this penal evolution and still use shock punishments. Even so, Foucault late in life irritated the left by some positive noises he made about the Iranian Revolution of 1979 which reinstated *Sharia* law and mandated judicial corporal punishment in Iran. The reality is Foucault traveled to Iran twice. His first visit was from September 16 to 24, 1978. During his stay in Iran, he met with a number of political figures, Shah's opposition and dissident clerics. His second stay was between November 9 and 15 in 1978, when he visited Tehran, Qom, and Abadan and met with the main leaders of the revolution. The result of his visits was a series of articles and reports which were published in the Italian newspaper, *Corriere della Sera.* His last report published in the newspaper on November 26, 1978, was titled "Khomeini is the Legendary Leader of the Iranian Revolution."[2] Formidable left intellectuals such as Maxime Rodinson and Simone de Beauvoir were not amused. Foucault did not give an explicit answer to these criticisms, and it was even thought that he implicitly reversed his position in his previous writings about Iran.

While a range of factors contribute to why countries employ shock punishment, retention is often linked to political stability and the rule of law. When secular criminal justice systems like the United States have undergone this penal evolution, they cannot reinstate it again, and judicial corporal punishment isn't appropriate for a liberal democracy.

This book is about two societies on both sides of the world, and two different systems of the criminal justice system. I do not mean to suggest these societies should adapt uniform aspects of the penal system. There is no reason to expect that other societies will all take the same turns. There is nothing inevitable about either the Iranian or American path. Not all societies necessarily evolve into countries with mild punishment practices. This claim would be false as the degradation process and practice of harsh punishments in contemporary Iran and other countries with Islamic criminal justice system demonstrate.

A harsh penal system that prioritizes degradation over mercy without considering the legal canon led us to conclude that may be punishment the way we want it. If not, there is certainly nothing to stop us from trying to overcome the traditions that have brought us to this point. In the United States in contrast to Iran, the abolition movement toward cruel and unusual punishment has been essentially religious.

The change in the penal systems of Iran and the United States seen in the light of international law could bring about real change in punishments by appealing to much grander cultural traditions. Punishment is not simply a legal administrative entity but also when David Garland called "an expression of state power, a statement of collective morality, a vehicle for emotional expression, an economically conditioned social policy, an embodiment of current sensibilities, and a set of symbols which display a cultural ethos and help create a social identity."[3]

The norm prohibiting cruel and unusual punishment is unique, because its interpretation is so closely related to public attitudes. What we really need to reestablish is the policy of punishment itself. It would be an exaggeration to suggest that mild punishment is coming soon in Iran or United States. Hopefully, authorities will continue to accept responsibility for policing penal systems where conditions reach subhuman levels.

The most severe punishment for the unsuccessful never deters the successful from repeating his crime, or even the potential miscreant from becoming a criminal. When the methods of punishment employed by the state are so efficient and certain that anyone thinking of committing a criminal offense is well aware that detection and consequent punishment are almost inevitable, the conquest of crime will be well on the way to accomplishment, but not before.

The United States locks up vast numbers of people for minor crimes and non-serious offenses, such as minor drug possession or infractions, and our criminal justice system wastes shocking amount of money on lengthy sentences for low-level offenders, and those offenders only become more and more crime-prone. If Americans are serious about reducing the incarceration rate and its costs, we can reinstate non-barbarous judicial corporal punishments such as shaming punishments, or launch an e-carceration system and electronic monitoring for our criminal justice system. This book didn't claim that judicial corporal punishment as implemented in Islamic criminal justice systems is the only solution to a broken prison system. Rather it argues contemporary use of judicial corporal punishment is barbaric and inappropriate for the standards of the twenty-first century. Thus, Islamic criminal justice systems with judicial corporal punishment need to be reformed and comply with the demands of modernity, and the United States and other secular criminal justice systems should not follow their path. As the Bible reminds us in Corinthian about the dilemmas of punishment, "Shall I come to you with a rod of discipline, or shall I come in love and with a gentle spirit?"[4]

NOTES

1. Peter Moskos, *In Defense of Flogging* (Basis Books, 2011).
2. Amir Fakhravar, *Comrade Ayatollah: Soviet KGB's Role in the Islamic Revolution and the Rise of Ali Khamenei to Power in Iran,* 200 (Los Angeles, CA: Ketab Publishing, 2016).
3. David Garland, *Punishment and Modern Society: A Study in Social Theory*, 287 (Oxford: Clarendon Press, 1990).
4. 1 Corinthians 4:21.

Appendix

Table of Cases

Aldridge v. Commonwealth, 2 Va.Cas. 447, 4 Va. 447, 1824 WL 1072, Va.Gen.Ct, June Term 1824.
Campbell & Cosans v. United Kingdom, 48 Eur. Ct. H.R. (ser. A) (1982).
Commonwealth v. Wyatt, 6 Rand. 694, 27 Va. 694, 1828 WL 860, Va.Gen. Ct, November Term 1828.
Cornell v. State, 74 Tenn. 624, 1881 WL 4276, 6 Lea 624, Tenn., April Term 1881.
Graham v. West Virginia, 224 U.S. 616 (1912).
Gregg v. Georgia, 428 U.S. 153, 183 (1976).
Ireland v. United Kingdom, 25 Eur. Ct. H.R. (ser. A) at 66 (1978).
McDonald v. Massachusetts, 180 U.S. 311 (1901).
Moore v. Missouri, 159 U.S. 673 (1895).
People v. Ferguson, 60 Mich. App. 302, 230 N.W.2d 406 (1975).
Stanford v. Kentucky, 492 U.S. 361, 369 (1989).
State v. Cannon, State v. Cannon, 190 A.2d 514 (Del. 1963).
State v. Farrow, 118 N.H. 296, 386 A.2d 808 (1978).
State v. Stetson, 317 So. 2d 172 (La. 1975).
Tyrer v. United Kingdom, 26 Eur. Ct. H.R. (ser. A) At 15, 17 (1978).
Workman v. Com., 429 S.W.2d 374, 33 A.L.R.3d 326 (Ky. 1968).

Glossary

Abolition: The act of officially ending or stopping something.

Achaemenian: Achaemenian dynasty (559–330 BCE) was an ancient Iranian dynasty whose kings founded and ruled the Achaemenian Empire. Probably the greatest of the Achaemenian rulers were Cyrus II (reigned 559–c.529 BCE), who actually established the empire and from whose reign it is dated; Darius I (522–486), who excelled as an administrator and secured the borders from external threats; and Xerxes I (486–465), who completed many of the buildings begun by Darius. During the time of Darius I and Xerxes I, the empire extended as far west as Macedonia and Libya and as far east as the Hyphasis (Beās) River; it stretched to the Caucasus Mountains and the Aral Sea in the north and to the Persian Gulf and the Arabian Desert in the south.

Addiction: Addiction is a complex condition, a brain disease that is manifested by compulsive substance use despite harmful consequences. In some criminal justice systems, addiction has been criminalized.

Adulterer: A person who has committed adultery.

Adultery: Crime of sexual relations between a married man with another woman other than his or her lawful spouse.

African Charter of Human Rights: The African Charter on Human and Peoples' Rights (also known as the Banjul Charter) is an international human rights instrument that is intended to promote and protect human rights and basic freedoms in the African continent.

Aggravating and Mitigating Factors: These factors can affect the outcome of a defendant's case in a good or bad way. Aggravating circumstances increase the severity and culpability of a crime. Mitigating factors decrease the severity and culpability of a crime.

Alcoholism: Alcoholism is an illness marked by consumption of alcoholic beverages at a level that interferes with physical or mental health, and social, family, or occupational responsibilities.

Aldridge v. Commonwealth: In 1824, the Virginia Supreme Court, in *Aldridge v. Commonwealth,* relied on the principle of separation of powers to uphold Virginia's legislation providing for the whipping of offenders.

Allameh Hilli: Hassan bin Sadid-Aldin was born on the 29th Ramadan of 648 A.H. He learned knowledge and philosophy from famous Iranian scientist of the seventh century "Khajeh Nasireddin-e Tousi." He was an eminent Twelver theologian who flourished under the Mongols in Iraq.

American Convention on Human Rights: American Convention on Human Rights is an international human rights instrument. It was adopted by many countries in the Western Hemisphere in San Jose, Costa Rica, on November 22, 1969.

Alternative Sentence: Alternative sentencing can refer to just about anything that isn't an outright sentence of incarceration. Some common sentencing alternatives include probation, community service, and even judicial corporal punishment.

Amnesty International: Amnesty International is an international nongovernmental organization focused on human rights, with its headquarters in the United Kingdom.

Amputation of hand: The common judicial punishment for theft in Islamic criminal justice systems. Amputation of the full length of four fingers of the right hand of the thief in such a manner that the thumb and palm of the hand remain.

Apostasy: The voluntary renunciation of Islam by a Muslim who converts to another faith, worships idols, or rejects any of the tenets of Islam by word, deed, or omission.

Appeal: The process of seeking a higher court's review of the lower court's decision for the purpose of correcting or changing the lower's court judgment or decision.

Avoidance of *Hudud* crimes in case of doubt: This Islamic legal maxim says that judges are to avoid imposing *hudud* punishments when beset by doubts as to the scope of the law or the sufficiency of the evidence.

Ayatollah: a title in the religious hierarchy in *shia* school of Islam achieved by scholars who have demonstrated highly advanced knowledge of Islamic law and religion.

Balser v. State (1963): In Balser, a defendant convicted of robbery challenged his sentence to twenty lashes as being constitutionally repugnant upon the same theories as were asserted by the defendant in State v. Cannon. The court summarily disposed of the issue, referring to its decision in State v. Cannon. Again, however, the whipping did not take place.

Beccaria: Cesare Beccaria is an Italian criminologist and economist. He is the father of classical school of criminology. He became an international celebrity in 1764 with the publication of *Crime and Punishment*, the first systematic statement of principles governing criminal punishment, in which he argued that the effectiveness of criminal justice depended more on the certainty of punishment than on its severity.

Bentham: Jeremy Bentham, jurist and political reformer, is the philosopher whose name is most closely associated with the foundational era of the modern utilitarian tradition.

Bodily harm: Bodily harm means any hurt or injury to a person that interferes with the health or comfort of the person and that is more than merely transient or trifling in nature.

Biblical flogging: Biblical flogging was limited to thirty-nine lashes and served as a metaphoric substitute for the death penalty.

Bill of Rights: The first ten amendments to the Constitution make up the Bill of Rights.

Bill of Rights of England: The English Bill of Rights was an act signed into law in 1689 by William III and Mary II, who became co-rulers in England after the overthrow of King James II. The bill outlined specific constitutional and civil rights and ultimately gave Parliament power over the monarchy.

Blasphemy: Irreverent behavior toward anything held sacred, such as cursing or reviling God.

Blood Money: Prescribes restitution or compensation for the victim in Islamic criminal justice systems.

Branding: Branding was an alternative when it was necessary to mark the criminal so that those who might have later dealings with him would be put on notice.

Breaking and entering: Breaking and entering is defined as entering a building through force without authorization.

Brutalizing effect: The brutalization hypothesis states that the harsh punishment lessens people's respect for laws, and legitimizes crime, which inadvertently leads to an increase in crime.

Canon law: Canon law refers to the body of ecclesiastical law that developed within Christianity, particularly Roman Catholicism, governing the internal hierarchy and administration of the church. It also governs church ceremonies, the role of clergy, religious education, discipline within the church, and any litigation falling within ecclesiastical jurisdiction. Canon law originated as a body of norms drawn from scripture, the decisions of ecclesiastical councils, rulings by the Pope (in the form of letters known as papal decretals), as well as secular Roman law.

Capital crime: Crimes punishable by death penalty.

Capital punishment: Capital punishment refers to the process of sentencing convicted offenders to death.

Castration: The process of removing the testicles of a male animal or human as a form of judicial corporal punishment.

Chemical castration: This type of castration has been used as a punishment against sex offenders.

Corporal punishment: Corporal punishment is the punishment of body. It is defined as "physical punishment as distinguished from pecuniary punishment or a fine; any kind of punishment of or inflicted on the body."

Commonwealth v. Wyatt (1828): The Virginia Supreme Court held that whipping was "odious but cannot be said to be *unusual.*"

Campbell & Cosans v. United Kingdom (1982): Campbell attended a school that disciplined students using corporal punishment. The Regional Education Council refused to guarantee that Campbell would not face such measures. Cosans also attended a school that used corporal punishment. He was to receive punishment for allegedly taking a prohibited shortcut through a cemetery on his way home from school.

Comparative Law: The scholarly study of the similarities and differences between the legal systems of different jurisdictions.

Convention against Torture: The Convention against Torture and Other Cruel, Inhuman or Degrading Treatment or Punishment (the "Torture Convention") is an international human rights treaty. It was adopted by the General Assembly of the United Nations on December 10, 1984.

Cornell v. State (1881): In addition, the Tennessee Supreme Court, in Cornell v. State, held, in 1881, that corporal punishment could be imposed, but only if sanctioned either by the legislature or a law or regulation made for the government of the convicts by the county court in due form, at a regular session, or the governing authorities of the corporate town by whom the workhouse has been established.

Corrections: Corrections refer to the supervision of persons arrested for, convicted of, or sentenced for criminal offenses. Correctional populations fall into two general categories: institutional corrections and community corrections. Correctional officers play a pivotal role in protecting public safety. They separate individuals convicted of crimes from communities as they serve out their sentences, and they also help those who have completed their sentences to live law-abiding lives through a variety of reentry services.

Corruption on earth crimes: Corruption on earth crimes have a vague definition. In Islamic criminal justice systems. Corruption on earth is not a crime, and its definition can be attributed to crimes that include waging war against the prophet and God, setting ablaze a mosque, destroying state property during internal rebellion and any criticism of state.

Council of Europe: The Council of Europe is the continent's leading human rights organization. It includes forty-six member states, twenty-seven of which are members of the European Union.

Crime: An act that violates criminal law and is punishable by criminal sanctions.

Crimes against persons: The term "crimes against the person" refers to a broad array of criminal offenses which usually involve bodily harm, the threat of bodily harm, or other actions committed against the will of an individual. Those involving bodily harm (or the threat thereof) include assault, battery, and domestic violence. Additionally, offenses such as harassment, kidnapping, and stalking also are considered crimes against the person.

Crimes against property: Property crimes include many common crimes relating to theft or destruction of someone else's property. They can range from lower-level offenses such as shoplifting or vandalism to high-level felonies including armed robbery and arson.

Crimes against public morals: These crimes include disorderly conduct, rioting, public indecency, vagrancy and loitering, gang activity, prostitution and solicitation, obscenity, and cruelty to animals. The crime of disorderly conduct punishes the disturbance of peace, public morals, or public decency.

Crimes against public order: A crime against public order, also known as a public safety crime, is a violation that interferes with the normal operations of society.

Criminal: Criminal is a popular term used for a person who has committed a crime or has been legally convicted of a crime.

Criminal Depopulation of Prisons: The criminal justice policy that focuses on reductions in prison and jail populations.

Criminal justice system: The interlocking network of law enforcement agencies, courts, and corrections institutions designed to enforce criminal law and protect society from criminal behavior.

Criminal law: Criminal law, as distinguished from civil law, is a system of laws concerned with crimes and the punishment of individuals who commit crimes.

Cross amputation: Amputation of right hand and left leg. This punishment has been prescribed by Islamic criminal justice systems.

Cruel and unusual punishment: Cruel and unusual punishment is a phrase mentioned in the Eighth Amendment of the US Constitution. Specifically, the Eighth Amendment prohibits cruel and unusual punishment. However, the Constitution does not give more guidance on that, and so courts—and particularly the Supreme Court—have heard a number of cases that have given guidance to the prohibition of cruel and unusual punishment.

Cultural relativism: Cultural relativism is used in international law to describe a "cultural chasm" in which irreconcilable cultural differences preclude the pervasive realization of substantive international law and morality. "Because all cultures are equal, according to this view, the human rights practices of different cultures must be equally tolerated."

Customary international law: Customary international law refers to international obligations arising from established international practices, as opposed to obligations arising from formal written conventions and treaties. Customary international law is a practice that is common among majority of nations.

Decriminalization: Decriminalization is the process through which the legislature removes criminal sanctions against an act, omission, article, or behavior which is considered a crime.

Defendant: Defendant, in criminal cases, is the person accused of the crime.

Derogatory punishment: Tending to lessen the merit or reputation of the offender by imposing a punishment.

Deterrence: Deterrence is the theory that punishments do not just punish violators, but also discourage other people from committing similar offenses. It is the strategy of preventing crime through the threat of punishment. Assumes that potential criminals will weight the costs of punishment versus the benefits of the criminal act; there, punishments should be served.

Detterent punishment: According to the deterrent theory, the main goal is to deter crime by inciting fear or setting an example for society.

Diyat (Blood Money)*:* Prescribes restitution or compensation for the victim in Islamic criminal justice systems.

Docking stool: The ducking stool was a device in which the prisoner was restrained and repeatedly dunked in water. The device itself was complicated to build and had to be built near a body of water sufficiently deep enough to submerge the victim. The necessity for a deep body of water conflicted with the desire that the punishment be in a central public place so that the greatest percentage of the community could view the spectacle.

Double jeopardy: Double jeopardy prohibits anyone from being prosecuted twice for substantially the same crime. The Fifth Amendment to the US Constitution prohibits a second prosecution for the same criminal offense.

Drug trafficking: Drug trafficking is the illegal transporting of or transacting of controlled substances.

Durkheim: Émile Durkheim was a French sociologist who rose to prominence in the late nineteenth and early twentieth centuries. Along with Karl Marx and Max Weber, he is credited as being one of the principal founders of modern sociology.

Eighth Amendment: The Eighth Amendment to the US Constitution provides that "cruel and unusual punishments" shall not be inflicted.

Enlightenment: A philosophical movement of the seventeenth and eighteenth centuries characterized by a belief in the power of human reason. This movement had a great impact on the development of criminal justice, particularly in the birth of the penitentiary.

European Convention on Human Rights: The European Convention on Human Rights (ECHR) protects the human rights of people in countries that belong to the Council of Europe.

Evidence: Anything that is used to prove the existence or non-existence of a fact.

Excessive punishment: An inhumane procedure that punishes a defendant too severely for any crime.

Ex post facto: Ex post facto is most typically used to refer to a criminal statute that punishes actions retroactively, thereby criminalizing conduct that was legal when originally performed.

Felony: In US law, a felony is typically defined as a crime punishable by a term of imprisonment of not less than one year or by the death penalty.

Fine: A fine is a penalty of money that a court of law or other authority decides to be paid as punishment for a crime.

Fiqh: or Islamic jurisprudence refers to the legal rulings of the Muslim scholars derived from the *Sharia.*

Flogging: Flogging is also known as whipping, lashing, strapping, beating, or caning. All these methods involve striking the accused with an object to produce immediate and acute pain. Various tools have been used to flog people including metal rods, straps, branches, logs, whips, rubber hoses, cat-o-nine tails, and rattan canes.

Foote v. State (1883): A defendant, sentenced to sixty days in jail and seven stripes for beating his wife, challenged the imposition of whipping as violative of the Eighth Amendment and its counterpart provision in the Maryland Constitution.

Fornication: Consensual sexual relations between two unmarried persons.

Fornicator: A person who has committed fornication.

Garcia v. Territory of New Mexico (1868): The Supreme Court of the Territory of New Mexico addressed the issue in Garcia v. Territory of New Mexico, where the court sentenced a mule thief to thirty stripes, as provided for by statute.

Ghāmidī: Javed Ahmad Ghamidi was born to a Sufi family in Panjab, Pakistan. His early education included secular schools, Arabic, and Persian. He then studied philosophy, English literature, and Islamic studies at Government College in Lahore. He actively studied under his most influential teacher Amīn Aḥsan Iṣlaḥī (1904–1997).

Gemara: The second part of the Talmud, consisting primarily of rabbinical analysis and commentary on the Mishnah.

Gregg v. Georgia (1976): Greg v Georgia is a US Supreme Court case in which it was held that death penalty for murder was not in and of itself a cruel and unusual punishment, and it reinstated the use of the death penalty in the United States.

Habitual offender: Habitual offender statutes, variously known as increased sentence statutes, enhanced punishment statutes, recidivist statute, and multiple offender statutes. These statutes require lengthy prison sentences for those who are convicted of multiple felonies.

Had theft*:* Theft is defined in *Sharia* as the act of taking other people's property without any lawful claim to it. Theft deprives a man of property. It is an encroachment upon the property of man without any justifiable society and is looked upon with terror. Therefore, strict measures have been ordered by the Islamic criminal justice system against thieves. The punishment for theft is in the Holy Quran: "As to the thief, male or female, cut off his or her hands as punishment by way of example from Allah for their crime. And Allah is exalted in power."

Hadith: Tradition of the Prophet or the Imams.

Halachic corporal punishment: Halachic corporal punishment, or flogging, was the standard form of punishment for crimes that did not have biblically prescribed penalties. There were two forms of flogging, biblical and rabbinic.

Hanging: Execution or by strangling or breaking the neck with a suspended noose.

Highway Robbery: Please refer to *Moharebeh.*

Homicide: Homicide is when one human being causes the death of another. Not all homicide is murder, as some killings are manslaughter, and some are lawful, such as when justified by an affirmative defense, like insanity or self-defense.

Hudud: Hudud or prescribed punishments are acts against God, and their prosecution is initiated by the state. They are absolute, universal, nonnegotiable, and unpardonable. For example, adultery and sodomy.

Human rights: Human rights are rights inherent to all human beings, regardless of race, sex, nationality, ethnicity, language, religion, or any other status.

Ijma: Consensus of opinions among Muslim Jurists.

Imprisonment: The act of confining a person in a penal institution such as a jail or prison for the purpose of serving a sentence imposed by a court.

Incapacitation: A strategy for preventing crime by detaining wrongdoers in prison, thereby separating them from the community and reducing criminal opportunities.

Incapacitative sanctions: Sanctions that confine individuals or limit their physical opportunities for criminal behavior.

Incarceration: Incarceration is the long-term confinement of convicted and sentenced offenders.

Incest: Incest is sexual intercourse between persons so closely related that they are forbidden by law to marry.

Indeterminate sentences: An indeterminate sentence is a type of custodial sentence that consists of a range of years (such as five to ten years) and not a fixed time, which means the convicted person's release date is left open.

Individualization of punishments: The individualization of punishment implies finding the balance between the gravity of the crime and the personality of the criminal, on one hand, and the punishment that will be applied, on the other hand. The governing principle of this procedure is, undoubtedly, the principle of proportionality.

Inflexibility of punishment: Applying unvarying punishments regardless of any sense of the individual deserts of offenders.

Injury: An injury is a harm suffered by a person due to some act or omission done by another person and can generally give rise to a tort claim or a criminal prosecution.

International Covenant on Civil and Political Rights (ICCPR): ICCPR is an international human rights treaty adopted by the United Nations in 1966.

International Human Rights: Human rights are "inalienable rights of all members of the human family." Thus, human rights are, in principle, applicable to every person, regardless of their nationality. The Universal Declaration gives an example of the substance of human rights agreements (although it is not itself a treaty, many nations have agreed to abide by its principles, and it serves as an inspiration for treaties on human rights).

International law: International law consists of rules and principles governing the relations and dealings of nations with each other, as well as the relations between states and individuals, and relations between international organizations. Public international law concerns itself only with questions of rights between several nations or nations and the citizens or subjects of other nations. In contrast, private international law deals with controversies between private persons. These controversies arise out of situations which have a significant relationship to multiple nations. In recent years the line between public and private international law has become increasingly uncertain. Issues of private international law may also implicate issues of public international law, and many matters of private international law have substantial international significance.

Intoxication: A state in which a person's normal capacity to act or reason is inhibited by alcohol or drugs.

Ireland v. United Kingdom: Ireland v. United Kingdom is a European Court of Human Rights (ECtHR) principally concerning the threshold at which "cruel and unusual treatment" becomes "torture" for the purposes of Article 3 of the European Convention on Human Rights (ECHR), and the circumstances in which an Article 15 "derogation in times of war or other public emergency" permit a valid deviation from the standards imposed by Article 5 (right to liberty and security) and Article 6 (right to a fair trial).

Islamic criminal justice system: When Islamic law or *Sharia* is the main source of a criminal justice system.

Islamic Declaration of Human Rights (1981): is a document created by Islamic Councils in Paris and London. It restates basic human rights using the language of Islamic jurisprudence.

Islamic state: Islamic states are Islamic nations in which *Sharia* law or Islamic law is a form of legislation.

Islamization: It refers to the process through which a society shifts toward Islamic law, and *Sharia* becomes the main source of the law.

Jafari School of Jurisprudence: Iran's legal school of thought is known as *Jafari* jurisprudence. It has been particularly influenced by the opinions of the sixth Imam, Abu Abdullah Jafar bin Mohammad Sadegh. According to the *Jafari* school, sources of Islamic law are the Holy Quran, tradition (*hadith*), the consensus of the jurist (*ijma*), and reason (*'aql*).

Judicial Corporal Punishment: Corporal punishment sentenced by a court.

Jurisdiction (of the court): Power of a court to adjudicate cases and issue orders.

Just deserts: This justification for punishment is appropriately called the principle of "just deserts." In the theory of "just deserts," both the offender and society benefit from the punishment.

Justice Brennan: He was an American lawyer and jurist who served as an Associate Justice of the US Supreme Court from 1956 to 1990 and known for being a leader of the US Supreme Court's liberal wing.

Justice Scalia: Antonin Gregory Scalia was an American jurist who served as an associate justice of the Supreme Court of the United States from 1986 until his death in 2016. He was an intellectual anchor for the originalist and textualist position in the US Supreme Court's conservative wing.

Justice Taylor: John Louis Taylor (March 1, 1769–January 29, 1829) was an American jurist and first chief justice of the North Carolina Supreme Court.

Legalization: Legalization refers to authentication or certification by an appropriate public authority. It is an act to make something lawful. It may also be called legitimation. For example, legalization of casino gambling refers to making casino gambling lawful; or legalization of assisted suicide refers to making assisted suicide lawful and legitimate, and legal consequences shall not follow a legitimate act.

Legislation: Legislation refers to the preparation and enactment of laws by a legislative body through its lawmaking process.

Life imprisonment: This is a prison sentence given to a convicted defendant in which they will remain in prison for their entire life.

Mandatory sentencing: Fixed sentences that take sentencing discretion out of the hands of judge.

Manslaughter: Manslaughter is an unlawful killing that doesn't involve malice aforethought intent to seriously harm or kill or an extreme, reckless disregard for life.

McDonald v. Massachusetts: Holding that a habitual criminal statute, "imposing a punishment on none but future crimes, is not ex post facto."

Marginal deterrence**:** It means an individual will be deterred from committing a more harmful act owing to the difference, or margin, between the expected sanction for it and for a less harmful act.

Massachusetts Body of Liberties (1641): Early Massachusetts colony law code inspired by Mosaic law.

Mishnah: Mishna is the first major written collection of the Jewish oral traditions which is known as the Oral Torah.

Minorities Declaration**:** Adopted by consensus in 1992, the purpose of the Declaration is the promotion and protection of the rights of persons belonging to national or ethnic, religious, and linguistic minorities and as such to contribute to the political and social stability of states in which they live.

Misdemeanor: A misdemeanor is a type of offense punishable under criminal law. A misdemeanor is typically a crime punishable by less than twelve months in jail.

Moen: Ole Martin Moen is another pro-judicial corporal punishment philosopher. Moen is a Norwegian philosopher at Oslo Metropolitan University. He believes "Incarceration," which is today's norm, also involves violence.

Moharebeh: Moharebeh or resorting to arms to frighten people is defined as an act of robbery by a group of armed men within the territory of the Islamic state that creates anarchy under which the property, privacy, safety, dignity, and religious values of the people would be violated. The crime is regarded as a war against God and his messenger. There are several alternative punishments for banditry, for instance execution, crucifixion, amputation of hand and foot, and exile (5:33, Surah Ma'ideh).

Montesquieu: Montesquieu was one of the great political philosophers of the Enlightenment. He constructed a naturalistic account of the various forms of government, and of the causes that made them what they were and that advanced or constrained their development. He used this account to explain how governments might be preserved from corruption. He saw despotism, in particular, as a standing danger for any government not already despotic and argued that it could best be prevented by a system in which different bodies exercised legislative, executive, and judicial power, and in which all those bodies were bound by the rule of law. This theory of the separation of powers had an enormous impact on liberal political theory, and on the framers of the Constitution of the United States of America.

Moral offenses: Moral offenses or crimes against morality are crimes that are considered to not have a victim when consenting adults are involved. Explore the definition and examples of crimes against morality, including prostitution, bigamy, pornography, illegal gambling, consensual sexual acts, and use of controlled substances.

Mosaheqeh: *Mosaheqeh* or lesbianism is female homosexuality. Punishment for lesbianism is one hundred (100) lashes for each party.

Moskos: Peter Moskos is an American professor at John Jay College of Criminal Justice. Peter Moskos makes the case that convicts should be given the option to choose corporal punishment as an alternative to incarceration.

Mutilation: There were three classes of punitive mutilation. First, where punishment mirrored the crime committed, the *lex talionis* method of punishment was administered. Mayhem was met with mayhem—an eye for an eye.

Newman: Graeme Newman is a distinguished professor emeritus at the School of Criminal Justice, University of Albany. Newman in his book *Just and Painful: A Case for the Corporal Punishment of Criminals* presents a reactionary alternative to the high-cost "schools of crime" we call prisons.

Official religion: Official religion is a religion or creed officially endorsed by a sovereign state.

Old Testament: Old Testament, the Hebrew Bible as interpreted among the various branches of Christianity. In Judaism, the Hebrew Bible is not only the primary text of instruction for a moral life but also the historical record of God's promise, first articulated in his covenant with Abraham, to consider the Jews his chosen people.

Organ retaliation: This punishment is based on the principle of eye for eye. Cutting off bodily organ or its injury if it were to be intentional is subject to retaliation in kind, and the wronged party is allowed for retaliation against the criminal based on the prescribed norms and religious judge's decree.

Parole: Parole is the conditional release of prisoners before they complete their sentence. Paroled prisoners are supervised by a public official, usually called a parole officer.

Penal code: The penal code of a country consists of all the laws that are related to crime and punishment.

Penal proportionality: The principle of proportional justice is used to describe the idea that the punishment of a certain crime should be in proportion to the severity of the crime itself.

Penitentiary prison: A penitentiary is a prison, especially a state or federal prison in the United States or Canada. Penitentiaries typically house criminals who have committed major crimes. The word is often used in formal contexts.

Penology: It is the division of criminology that concerns itself with the philosophy and practice of society in its efforts to repress criminal activities. The focus of penology is the study of punishments.

Petty crimes: A type of crime that is not considered serious when compared with some other crimes, such as shoplifting.

Petty larceny: Petty larceny or petty theft (commonly spelled petit larceny) is a term used to describe thefts where the value of the property taken is low.

Political crimes: The political criminal is defined as an individual who, motivated by his conviction, commits an unlawful act designed to attack the social structure to bring about a reorganization of the system.

Pretrial detention: Pretrial detention, also known as remand or preventative detention, is when someone is detained by the state while they are waiting for a trial to determine whether they are innocent or guilty of a crime.

Principal punishment: Principal penalties are those imposed independently. For each crime, the court can only apply one principal penalty.

Prison: Prison is an institution for the confinement of persons who have been remanded (held) in custody by a judicial authority or who have been deprived of their liberty following conviction for a crime. A person found guilty of a felony or a misdemeanor may be required to serve a prison sentence.

Prison overcrowding: Prison overcrowding is a consequence of criminal justice policy not of rising crime rates and undermines the ability of prison systems to meet basic human needs, such as healthcare, food, and accommodation.

Probation: Considered the oldest form of noninstitutional corrections, its development in the United States is credited to the efforts of John Augustus in Boston in the 1840s.

Prostitution: Prostitution involves engaging, agreeing, or offering to engage in sexual conduct with another person in return for a fee.

Public punishment: Public punishment is a form of punishment whose main feature is dishonoring or disgracing an offender in a public place.

Punishment: A penalty is the punishment imposed upon a person who has violated the law.

Punitive: Concerned with inflicting punishment.

Punitive amputation: This is the punishment for *had* theft. Islamic criminal justice systems mandate as to the thief, male or female, cut off his or her hands as punishment.

Puritans: A religious movement that sought to purify the church of England.

Quakers: A radical religious sect that emerged in seventeenth-century England. They would play an important role in various criminal justice reform efforts in America beginning from colonial Pennsylvania.

Qadhf: Qadhf or false accusation of unlawful intercourse is prohibited under *Sharia* law and it's punishable by flogging.

Qisas: Qisas or retaliation is another class of crime in Islamic criminal justice systems which involve lethal acts against the person (homicide) and nonlethal offenses against the body (e.g., assaults, maiming).

Rabbinic whipping: Rabbinic whipping served to discipline an offender who had flouted a rabbinic precept and was not limited to a specific number of lashes. Theoretically, a candidate for rabbinic whipping could be flogged to death.

Rajm: The punishment of stoning to death in Islamic criminal justice systems.

Rape: The crime of rape—often referred to as sexual assault—generally refers to non-consensual sexual acts that are either committed by physical force, threat of injury, or other duress, or committed against people who are legally or otherwise unable to consent. The antiquated common law definition of rape was unlawful intercourse by a man against a woman who is not his wife, by force or threat, and against her will. However, most states have revised and broadened the definition of rape so that marriage, gender, and force are no longer relevant; The victim's lack of consent is the crucial element. A lack of consent can include the victim's inability to provide consent (functionally or legally) due to age, mental disability, or even the effects of drugs or alcohol.

Ratification: Ratification defines the international act whereby a state indicates its consent to be bound to a treaty if the parties intended to show their consent by such an act. In the case of bilateral treaties, ratification is usually accomplished by exchanging the requisite instruments, while in the case of multilateral treaties the usual procedure is for the depositary to collect the ratifications of all states, keeping all parties informed of the situation. The institution of ratification grants states the necessary time frame to seek the required approval for the treaty on the domestic level and to enact the necessary legislation to give domestic effect to that treaty.

Recidivism: Recidivism is measured by criminal acts that resulted in rearrest, reconviction, or return to prison with or without a new sentence during a three-year period following the person's release.

Red Hannah: Delaware's whipping device.

Rehabilitation: The idea that the purpose of punishment is to apply treatment and training to the offender so that he is made capable of returning to society and functioning as a law-abiding member of the community.

Reintegration: A goal of corrections that focuses on preparing the offender or a return to the community.

Religious law: Religious law refers to ethical and moral codes taught by religious traditions. Examples include Christian canon law, Islamic *Sharia*, Jewish halakha, and Hindu law. The two most prominent systems, canon law and *Sharia*, differ from other religious laws in that canon law is the codification of Catholic, Anglican, and Orthodox law as in civil law, while *Sharia* derives many of its laws from juristic precedent and reasoning by analogy.

Retaliation: It means any act of harm committed in response to an actual or perceived harm.

Retribution: One of the oldest and most basic justifications for punishment involves the principles of revenge and retribution.

Retributive theory: A response to criminal behavior that focuses on the punishment of lawbreakers and the compensation of victims. In general, the severity of the punishment is proportionate to the seriousness of the crime.

Retributivism: Retributivism is a policy or theory of criminal justice that advocates the punishment of criminals in retribution for the harm they have inflicted.

Rehabilitative system: When the focus of criminal justice system is on rehabilitation of criminals instead of harsh punishments.

Robbery: The unlawful taking of property from the person of another through the use of threat or force.

Scarre: Among philosophers, Geoffrey Scarre defends judicial corporal punishment, on utilitarian grounds. He argues corporal punishment is not inevitably crueler or demanding than conventionally proffered punitive methods and that consideration should be given to its limited experimental reintroduction.

Sanhedrin: The Supreme Court of ancient Israel.

Sassanian: Sassanian dynasty was ancient Iranian dynasty that ruled an empire (224–651 CE), rising through Ardashir I's conquests in 208–224 CE and destroyed by the Arabs during the years 637–651. Under the leadership of Ardashīr (reigned as "king of kings" 224–241), the Sasanians overthrew the Parthians and created an empire that was constantly changing in size as it reacted to Rome and Byzantium to the west and to the Kushans and Hephthalites to the east. At the time of Shapur I (reigned 241–272), the empire stretched from Sogdiana and Iberia (Georgia) in the north to the Mazun region of Arabia in the south and extended to the Indus River in the east and to the upper Tigris and Euphrates river valleys in the west.

Secular Islamic state: Secular Islamic state in which government institutions are separated from the role of religion.

Sentence: A criminal sentence refers to the formal legal consequences associated with a conviction.

Sex Crimes: A number of different offenses fall into the sex crimes category, but they generally involve illegal or coerced sexual conduct against another individual. Every state has laws against prohibiting the various types of sex crimes, such as rape and sexual assault, and each state has its own time limit (or "statute of limitations") in which victims of sex crimes may file a lawsuit against the alleged offender. People convicted of sex crimes, regardless of severity, are considered "sex offenders" by their respective states and face having their names added to state and federal sex offender registries. In Islamic criminal justice systems, consensual sexual crimes are included in this category as well.

Shaming punishments: An ancient form of exhibitory punishment that can include letter-wearing or public humiliation. Several judges have used this as an alternative to prison sentences in the United States in recent years.

Sharia: The *Sharia*, general and particular rules of Islamic corpus juris, is not merely a code of law but a code of conduct of behavior and ethics, a combination of law and morality, one and inseparable. *Sharia* was developed in the centuries following Prophet Mohammed's death in 632, and its formulation was essentially complete by the thirteenth century.

Shaykh Mufid: Abu 'Abd Allah Muhammad ibn Muhammad ibn al-Nu'man al-'Ukbari al-Baghdadi known as Shaykh Mufid for his expertise in philosophical theology (c. 948–1022 CE) was an eminent Twelver Shi'a theologian.

Shiite: Shiites are the second-largest branch of Islam, after Sunnis. A *shiite* believes that Mohammed's son-in-law, Ali, was his legitimate successor as political and religious leader. Though *shiites* hold this basic belief in common, there are further divisions within *shia* Islam, another name for the group of *shiites*.

Shooting (firing squad): Execution by shooting is a method of capital punishment in which a person is shot to death by one or more firearms.

Shoplifting: Theft is the taking of another person's personal property with the intent of depriving that person of the use of their property. Also referred to as larceny. Theft is often divided into grand theft and petty theft.

Slander: A false statement, usually made orally, which defames another person.

Sodomy laws: Sodomy laws criminalize consensual intercourse between two males.

Stanford v. Kentucky: Judge Rehnquist, writing his plurality opinion, stated neither norms nor the legal standards of other countries should disposition the Eighth Amendment. The government believes domestic laws provide more protection than international treaties and customary laws. Furthermore, even if the United States were to adopt the international definition of torture, application of this norm to lawful sanctions may be inappropriate.

State religion: State religion is an Islamic country in which Islam is the official religion of a country, and Islamic courts may be used.

State v. Canon: case in which the Court held compacts for sexual non-intercourse, easily made and easily broken, when the prior marriage relations continue to exist, with the occupation of the same house and table and the keeping up of the same family unity, is not a lawful substitute for the monogamous family which alone the statute tolerates

State v. Stetson: This case is about conviction for distribution of heroin by Richard Stetson. He was sentenced to life imprisonment. In a dual attack upon this prosecution, by motions to quash, Stetson alleges that he was denied due process of law and a fair trial because he was not arrested until seven months after the alleged sale of narcotics; and the mandatory life imprisonment prescribed by statute is cruel and unusual punishment.

Stocks and pillory: The stock held prisoners in a seated position with their legs and hands secured. The pillory held the prisoner in a standing position with head and hands secured in a locked frame. Offenders were subject to public ridicule, pelting, and stoning while held in either the stock or the pillory. In some cases, the prisoner received an additional form of punishment, such as flogging or branding, while he was confined to the stock or the pillory.

Status crime: Offenses have traditionally been defined in terms of acts or failure to act. Despite the general rule that in order to be considered a crime, an act must be one that is prohibited or recognized as a failure to act, certain atypical offenses are defined in terms of personal status or condition of being rather than in terms of the acts committed—for example, being a vagrant, prostitute, drunkard, gambler, beggar, narcotic addict, or homosexual.

Sunnah: Tradition of Prophet Mohammad.

Taazir: Taazir or discretionary punishment means to prevent, to respect, and to reform. In the Islamic legal context, *taazir* is defined as follows: discretionary punishment to be delivered for transgressions against God, or against individuals for which there is neither fixed punishment nor penance.

Talmudic law: refers to the central text of Rabbinic Judaism and the primary source of Jewish religious law (halakha) and Jewish theology.

Theft: Theft is the taking of another person's personal property with the intent of depriving that person of the use of their property. Also referred to as larceny. Theft is often divided into grand theft and petty theft.

Tyrer v. United Kingdom: The continental judges of European Court of Human Rights were shocked at the practice of birching, but Judge Fitzmaurice was not at all outraged. Because he was educated under a system according to which the corporal punishment of schoolboys was regarded as the normal sanction for serious or even less serious misbehavior.

United Nations Office on Drugs and Crime: The agency's focus is the trafficking in and abuse of illicit drugs, crime prevention and criminal justice, international terrorism, and political corruption.

Universal Declaration of Human Rights (1948): The Universal Declaration of Human Rights (UDHR) is a document that acts like a global road map for freedom and equality—protecting the rights of every individual, everywhere. It was the first time countries agreed on the freedoms and rights that deserve universal protection in order for every individual to live their lives freely, equally, and in dignity.

Utilitarian: The doctrine that an action is right insofar as it promotes happiness and that the greatest happiness of the greatest number should be the guiding principle of conduct.

Vagrancy: Historically, vagrancy laws made it a crime for a person to wander from place to place without visible means of support. Basically, these laws criminalized being homeless and jobless. Historically, vagrancy laws made it a crime for a person to wander from place to place without visible means of support.

Vienna Convention on the Law of Treaties (1969): The Vienna Convention on the Law of Treaties is an international agreement regulating treaties between states. Known as the "treaty on treaties," it establishes comprehensive rules, procedures, and guidelines for how treaties are defined, drafted, amended, interpreted, and generally operated.

Victimless crime: A victimless crime is a crime that has no direct victim, causes no direct harm to a third party, and involves one or more consenting adults. For example, adultery or sodomy in Islamic criminal justice systems.

Werner v. State (1884): In Werner, the Court held: Corporal punishment by the lash can be inflicted lawfully upon the convicts in the penitentiary for refusal to work, only under a rule or regulation made for that purpose by the board of commissioners; for all questions of discipline are deferred to their discretion by the legislature, and it follows that the manner of punishment to be inflicted by way of correction must be prescribed by them.

Whipping: Whipping is also known as flogging, lashing, strapping, beating, or caning. All these methods involve striking the accused with an object to produce immediate and acute pain. Various tools have been used to flog people including metal rods, straps, branches, logs, whips, rubber hoses, cat-o-nine tails, and rattan canes.

Wine drinking: Punishment for wine drinking during the time of the Holy Prophet was beating with shoes, sticks, and hands without specifying the number of lashes.

Workman v. Com: In Workman, the Commonwealth had agreed to dismiss the indictment if Workman submitted to and passed a polygraph examination administered by the Kentucky State Police. Workman apparently took and passed three examinations, at least one of which was requested by the Commonwealth's Attorney and conducted by the State Police. Workman moved the trial court to enforce the bargain and dismiss the indictment, providing affidavits and test results.

Zoroastrian Religion: The ancient Persian religion founded by Prophet Zoroaster espoused the worship of the daily Ormazd in the context of a universal struggle between the forces of light and of darkness.

Bibliography

Alasti, Sanaz. "Comparative study of cruel & unusual punishment for engaging in consensual homosexual acts: In international Conventions, the United States and Iran." *Annual Survey of International & Comparative Law* 12 (2006): 149–269.

Alasti, Sanaz. "Comparative study of stoning punishment in the religions of Islam and Judaism." *Justice Policy Journal* 4, no. 1 (2007): 1–38.

Alasti, Sanaz, and Eric Bronson. "Corrections in Iran." *The Encyclopedia of Corrections* 1 (2017): 1–5.

Alasti, Sanaz and Eric Bronson. "Crime and Punishment in Iran (Islamic Republic of)," in *The Encyclopedia of Crime and Punishment*, 1–5. Wiley-Blackwell (2015).

Alasti, Sanaz. *Cruel and Unusual Punishment: Comparative Perspective in International Conventions, the United States and Iran*, 57. Florida: Vandeplas (2008).

Alperin, Howard. Length of Sentence as Violation of Constitutional Provisions Prohibiting Cruel and Unusual Punishment, 33 ALR3d.

Amin, Hassan. *The History of Law in Iran.* Tehran, Iran: The Encyclopedia of Iran Publications (2004).

Anderson, J.N.D. "Homicide in Islamic law." *Bulletin of the School of Oriental & African Studies* 13 (1951): 811, 815.

Anderson, J.N.D. "Law as a social force in Islamic culture and history." *Bulletin of SOAS* 20 (1957): 13–40.

Arafa, Mohamed and Jonathan Burns. "Judicial corporal punishment in the United States? Lessons from Islamic criminal law for curing the ills of mass incarceration." *Indiana International & Comparative Law Review* 25 (2015): 385.

Bahrami, Mohammad. "Islamic jurisprudence and legal analysis of hudoud punishments are to be prevented in case of doubt." *Legal viewpoints Journal* 5 (1376 Solar Hejira) [In Farsi].

Bahrampour, Firouzeh. "Note and comment: The canning of Michael Fay: Can Singapore's punishment withstand the scrutiny of international law." *Am. U.J. International Law & Policy* 10 (1995): 1057.

Baldwin, Simeon. "The restoration of whipping as a punishment for crime." *Green Bag* 13 (1901): 65, 66.
Bambale, Yunesa. *Crimes and Punishments under Islamic Law*. Malthouse Press Limited (2003).
Bassiouni, Cherif. *Introduction to Islam*. Rand McNally & Company (1988).
Bassiouni Cherif and Gamal Badr. "The Shariah: Sources, interpretation and rule-making." *UCLA Journal of Islamic & Near Eastern Law* 1 (2002).
Beccaria, Cesarre. *On Crimes and Punishments*, Translated with an introduction by Henry Paolucci. Indianapolis: Bobbs-Merrill (1963).
Bentham, Jeremy. *Principles of Penal Law*, in The Works of Jeremy Bentham 365, 401 (John Bowring ed., 1843).
Bradford, William, "An enquiry how far the punishment of death is necessary in Pennsylvania." *American Journal of Legal History* 12 (1968).
Bukhari; Mohammad Ibn Esmaeil; *Sahih Bokhari, vol.* 6, Hadith No. 25. Lebanon: Dar 'Fekr Publication (1401 Lunar Hejiri) [In Arabic].
Caldwell, Robert Graham. *Criminology*, 451–52 (2d ed. 1965).
Caldwell, Robert Graham. *Red Hannah, Delaware Whipping Post*. University of Philadelphia Press, pp. 69–82(1947).
Compbell, James. "Revival of the eight amendment: Development of cruel-punishment doctrine by the supreme court." *Stanford Law Review* 16 (July 1964): 996.
Ebrahimi, Eesa. "Philosophy of punishment in Islam." *Bar Association Journal* 38 (1333): Solar Hejira [In Farsi].
Emmerson, B and A. Ashworth. *Human Rights and Criminal Justice*. London: Sweet & Maxwell (2001).
Fakhravar, Amir. *Comrade Ayatollah: Soviet KGB's Role in the Islamic Revolution and the Rise of Ali Khamenei to Power in Iran*. Los Angeles, CA: Ketab Publishing (2016).
Fitzpatrick, Joan and Alice Miller. "International standards on the death penalty: Shifting discourse." *Brooklyn Journal of International Law* 19 (1993): 273, 278.
Garland, David. *Punishment and Modern Society: A Study in Social Theory*. Oxford: Clarendon Press (1990).
Ghāmidī, Jāved Aḥmad. *Hudūd and Discretionary Punishment: A Few Important Points*, in Burhān (Proof), 7th ed. Lahore: al-Mawrid (2009).
Ghāmidī, Jāved Aḥmad. Qayd kī sazā (Prison as Punishment), Ishrāq (July 1989).
Goldouzian, Iraj. *Special Criminal Law*. Tehran, Iran: Mizan Publication (1999) [In Farsi].
Gorji, Abolghasem. *Legal Injunctions of the Quran*. Iran, Tehran: Mizan Publication (2004).
Hall, Daniel. "When canning meets the eighth amendment: Whipping offenders in the United States." *Widenr Journal of Public Law* 4 (1995): 403.
Hatfield, Steven A. "Criminal punishment in America: From the colonial to the modern era." *USAF Academic Journal of Legal Studies* 1 (1990): 139.
Hutington, Samuel. "The clash of civilizations?" *FOREIGN AFF* (Summer 1993): 22–25.
Israel, Drapkin. *Crime and Punishment in the Ancient World*. Lexington Books (1989).

Javan, Mosa; *Zoroaster Laws or Vandidad of Zoroaster's Holy Book.* Iran, Tehran: Donyayeh Ketab (1953) [In Farsi].

Joyner Christopher C. and John C. Dettling. "Bridging the cultural chasm: Cultural relativism and the future of international law." *California Western International Law Journal* 20 (1990): 275.

Kamali, Mohammed Hashim. *Principles of Islamic Jurisprudence.* Paul & Co Pub Consortium (1989).

Kan, Steven S. "Corporal punishments and optimal incapacitation." *Journal of Legal Studies* 25 (January, 1996): 121.

Karami, Mohammad Bagher. *Introduction on Criminal Justice System in Ancient Iran.* Khate sevvom (1380) [in Farsi].

Lacey, Forrest. "Vagrancy and other crimes of personal condition." *Harvard Law Review* 66 (May 1953).

Ledbetter, Garry. "The international norms: An interpretation of the "Evolving Standard of Decency."" *San Diego Justice Journal* 2 (1994): 263.

Lewicki, Edna. "Need word's collide: The Hudad crimes of Islamic law and international human rights." *NYILR* 13 (2000): 43.

Ledewitz, Bruce S., and Scott Staples. "Reflections on the Talmudic and American death penalty." *University of Florida: Journal of Law & Public Policy* 6 (1993): 33.

Lippman, Matthew, Sean McConville, and Mordechai Yerushalmi. *Islamic Criminal Law and Procedure: An Introduction.* New York: Praeger Publication (1988).

Latzer, Barry. *Myth of Overpunishment: A Defense of the American Justice System and a Proposal to Reduce Incarceration While Protecting the Public.* Republic Book Publishing (2022).

Manley, Steven. "The constitution, the punishment of death, and misguided originalism." *L. Rev. M.S.U. D.C.L.* 1999 (1999): 913.

Mirza Ghomi, Abolghasem. *Jame al-shetat* (Vol, 1), Keyhan Publication (1992).

Moen, Ole Martin. "Judicial corporal punishment." *Journal of Ethics & Social Philosophy* 17 (2020): 27.

Montazeri, Hossein Ali. *Tozihol al-masayel.* Tehran, Iran: Fekr Publication (1998).

Morse, Alice Earle. *Curious Punishments of Bygone Days.* Chicago: Herbert S. Stone and Company (1896).

Moskos, Peter. *In Defense of Flogging.* Basic Books (2011).

Newman, Graeme. *Just and Painful: A Case for the Corporal Punishment of Criminals.* Macmillan Publishing Company (1983).

O'Hanlon, Ann. *New Interest in Corporal Punishment.* Wash. Post (Mar. 5, 1995).

Ownes, Emily. *Religion and the Death Penalty.* William Eerdmans Publishing Company (2004).

Page, Drew. "Cruel and unusual punishment and sodomy statutes: The breakdown of the Soldem v. Helm." *University of Chicago Law Review* 56 (1989): 367.

Parr, Stephen. "A new perspective on the cruel and unusual punishment clause." *Tennessee Law Review* 68 (2000): 41.

Paust, Jordan J. "Human dignity as a constitutional right: A jurisprudentially based inquiry into criteria and content." *Howard Law Journal* 27 (1984): 145, 176.

Powers, Edwin. *Crime and Punishment in Early Massachusetts: 1620–1692*. Boston: Beacon Press (1966).

Ramadan, Tarigh. *New Directions in Islamic Thought: Exploring Reform and Muslim Tradition*. I.B. Tauris & Co. Ltd (2009).

Ravandi, Morteza. *Revolution of Law and Administration of Justice*. Tehran, Iran (1988) [In Farsi].

Robertson, James. "Houses of the dead: Warehouse prisons, paradigm change, and the Supreme Court." *Houston Law Review* 34 (1997): 1003.

Roth, Mitchel P. *An Eye for an Eye: A Global History of Crime and Punishment*. London, UK: Reaktion Books Ltd. (2014).

Roth, Mitchel P. *Crime and Punishment: A History of the Criminal Justice System*. California: Thomson Wadsworth (2005).

Sanders, Scott. "Scarlet letters, Bilbo's and cable TV: Are shame punishments cruel and unusual or are they viable option for American jurisprudence?" *Washburn Law Journal* 37 (1998): 359.

Saneiee, Parviz. *General Criminal Law*. Iran, Tehran: Ganje Danesh Publication (Fall 1992).

Scarre, Geoffrey. "Corporal punishment." *Ethical Theory & Moral Practice* 6, no. 3 (2003).

Schabas, William A. *The Death Penalty as Cruel Treatment and Torture*. Northeastern University Press (1996).

Schabas, William A. "Symposium: religion's role in the administration of the death penalty Islam and the death penalty." *William & Mary Bill of Rights Journal* 9 (2000): 223.

Schacht, Joseph. "Problems of modern Islamic legislation." *Studia Islamica* 12 (1960): 99.

Schneider, Irene. "Imprisonment in pre-classical and classical Islamic law." *Islamic Law and Society* 2, no. 2 (1995).

Shuster, Kenneth. "Halacha as a model for American penal practice: A comparison of Halachic and American punishment methods." *Nova Law Review* 19 (1995): 965.

Sinah, Surya Prakash. *Legal Polycentricity and International Law*. California Academic Press (1996).

Spierenburg, Pieter. *The Body and the State, in The Oxford History of the Prison*, Norval Morris & David J. Rothman eds. (1995).

Starkweather, David A. Note. "The retributive theory of "Just Deserts" and victim participation in plea bargaining." *Indiana Law Journal* 67 (1992): 853, 854–855.

Stephen, James F. *History of the Criminal Law of England* (Making of the British Legal System). Routledge/Thoemmes P; 1 edition (December 4, 1996).

Tubb, Kristin O'Donnell. *Freedom from Cruel and Unusual Punishment*. Greenhaven Press (2005).

Vahedi, Ava. *Criminal Justice System of Iran in Sassanian Era*. Tehran, Iran: Mizan Publication (2001) [In Farsi].

Whiteman, James. *Harsh Justice: Criminal Punishment and the Widening divide between America and Europe*. New York: Oxford University Press (2003).

Wiedeman, Whitney. "Special issue: Juvenile justice and the criminal law: Comment: Don't spare the rod: A proposed return to public, corporal punishment on convicts." *American Journal of Criminal Law* 23 (1996): 651.

Wyman, James H. "Vengeance is whose? The death penalty and cultural relativism in international law." *Journal of Transnational Law and Policy* (Summer 1997).

Zafari, Mohammadreza. *Origins of Criminal Justice in Islamic Law*. Tehran, Iran: Amirkabir Publication (1997) [In Farsi].

Index

About the Author

Dr. Sanaz Alasti is professor of criminal justice and director of the Center for Death Penalty Studies at Lamar University. She has completed her post-doctorate at Harvard Law School. Alasti has published ten books and several peer-reviewed articles on various aspects of the criminal justice system. She has researched, written about, and made presentations about the death penalty and other harsh punishments for the past twenty years. Dr. Alasti founded the Center for Death Penalty Studies in 2013. She has made significant research contributions to the study of comparative criminal justice systems and on the role of religion in the punishment of crime. In 2012, she has been invited to Italy as a lecturer to provide instruction to military officers, legal advisors, and political and policy advisors on *Sharia* law at a seminar hosted by NATO School, and in the summer of 2015, she has been invited to organize a conference with the attendance of prestigious law professors from Harvard, NYU, and UC Berkeley for "Onati International Institute for the Sociology of law" in Spain. Her interviews have been featured in magazines such as the *New Yorker*, the *Examiner*, and the Law Library of Congress website.

www.ingramcontent.com/pod-product-compliance
Ingram Content Group UK Ltd.
Pitfield, Milton Keynes, MK11 3LW, UK
UKHW041839031026
15587UKWH00002B/889

9 781666 930290